The Street Children *of* DICKENS'S LONDON

The Street Children *of* DICKENS'S LONDON

HELEN AMY

AMBERLEY

First published 2012

Amberley Publishing
The Hill, Stroud
Gloucestershire GL5 4EP

www.amberley-books.com

British Library Cataloguing in Publication Data.
A catalogue record for this book is available from the British Library.

ISBN 978 1 84868 846 9

Typeset in 10pt on 12pt Sabon.
Typesetting and Origination by Amberley Publishing.
Printed in the UK.

Contents

List of Illustrations

Introduction

This book tells the story of the vast number of children who spent most of their time living and working on the streets of Victorian London. It is about their daily lives, their homes and backgrounds, and how they survived. It is also about the problem their presence posed as London was transformed into a grand imperial capital city and how this problem was eventually solved.

Some children who spent long hours on the streets belonged to the respectable 'industrious poor' class. The majority, however, were outcast members of the 'underclass', the very lowest stratum of society. It is these children who are the subject of this book and to whom the term 'street children' will refer throughout. They survived by working on the streets, begging, crime, prostitution, or a combination of these methods. These children also included those caring for other children – the 'little mothers' – and those roaming the streets unsupervised. Before their story can be told, however, the street children need to be placed into their historical context.

The poor of Victorian England, of whom the street children formed a part, were separated from the rich by an enormous gulf. In his novel *Sybil,* published in 1845, Benjamin Disraeli described the 'two nations' of the rich and poor. He stated that there was 'no intercourse and no sympathy' between them and that they were 'as ignorant of each other's habits, thoughts and feelings, as if they were inhabitants of different planets; who are formed by different breeding, fed by different food, ordered by different manners and governed by different laws'.

Britain was the world's richest and most advanced industrial nation. The poor, however, most of whom lived in towns and cities, had not benefited from this success and the resulting prosperity, despite the fact that many had contributed to it. Fluctuating economic conditions throughout the nineteenth century made life uncertain and desperately hard for the poorest classes. The period known as the 'hungry forties' was a particularly bad time. Industry failed, unemployment was high and food was expensive. The Repeal of the Corn Laws in 1846 and the resulting reduction in the price of bread helped the poor. The 1860s were more settled economically but further trade depressions occurred in the last three decades of the century.

Throughout the Victorian period there were rumblings of discontent among the lower classes. In the 1840s this manifested itself in Chartist agitation with demands for political reform, including the introduction of universal manhood suffrage. This eventually faded out but contributed to middle-class fears that the working classes would rise up and rebel against their lot in life. This fear of unrest dated back to the French Revolution at the end of the eighteenth century. Uprisings in continental cities in 1848 added to tension and uneasiness regarding the poor.

At this time it was believed that the poor were to blame for their own poverty due to such characteristics as laziness, fecklessness and thriftlessness. They were not seen as victims of circumstances beyond their control and the environment they were forced to live in. The Victorians believed that everyone had their place in the social pyramid, from the queen at the top to the poorest citizens at the bottom. It was also believed that each person's place in society was ordained by God, a concept which rather contradicted the belief that the poor were to blame for their own plight.

The idea that the poor were responsible for their own misfortune underpinned the Poor Law Amendment Act of 1834 which divided the poor into the deserving and the undeserving. Under the Act 'outdoor relief' was abolished and the only help available for the poor was 'indoor relief' in the workhouse. Conditions inside workhouses were deliberately made worse than the living conditions of the poorest workers outside to deter the idle from seeking relief. Consequently, only the truly desperate entered the grim new union workhouses, which soon came to be known as 'bastilles'. The only help for the poor, apart from that available in the workhouse, was provided by charity and the Church. The government, which believed that its role was confined to keeping the peace and defending the realm, followed a policy of 'laissez-faire', or non-intervention, regarding social problems. This policy was maintained by successive governments well into the later Victorian period.

As a result of government policy, including the harsh Poor Law, many of the poorest and most vulnerable people, including children, ended up living on the streets of towns and cities. One reason why so many children were victims of poverty was that the population of Victorian England was predominantly young. One person in three was under fifteen of years of age, despite the high mortality rate in this age group.

The gulf between the rich and poor was nowhere more apparent than in London. The population of the capital rose at an unprecedented and alarming rate throughout the nineteenth century due to immigration from abroad and other parts of Britain. People had been drawn to London for centuries by its attractions as the capital city. This migration from other parts of Britain, especially rural areas, rose considerably following the Industrial Revolution as people searched for work. There was not enough work in London, however, for all those who sought it and those who were lucky enough to find a job were poorly paid. There was also not enough housing to accommodate London's burgeoning population or a strong enough infrastructure to support it.

In London the rich and the poor came into daily contact on the streets, in the market places and in some leisure venues. In some parts of the capital they lived close to each other but, despite their close proximity, few of the better-off Londoners had any idea how their poorest fellow citizens lived. Only the clergy and charity workers ever ventured into the many slum districts of the capital. 'Outcast London', as the abject poor were termed, included many of the children who spent most of their time living and working on the streets. These ragged, dirty, hungry children gave the impression that hordes of feral urchins infested the streets of London. This impression was unfair, however, because a considerable proportion of these children, despite appearances, came from good, caring families and were polite, well-behaved, hard-working and were doing their best against impossible odds to survive by honest means. Nevertheless, the street children tended to be lumped together as an undesirable and threatening presence; they were seen as a blight on the greatest and richest city in the world. Their presence became more embarrassing as the century progressed and London was improved and modernised into a grand imperial capital city.

Poor children had to work in order to survive in Victorian England, either to contribute to their family's income or to support themselves if they were alone. Many families were so poor that even the small amount that a very young child could earn made a difference to their chances of survival. Poverty forced the poor to regard their offspring as little more than economic units and their employers viewed them as cheap, expendable labour. Children worked in factories, mines, foundries, brickyards, dustyards, sweat-shops, home-working trades, as domestic servants and on the streets. It was considered perfectly acceptable for poor children to work and, even though legislation was eventually introduced to improve the working conditions and reduce the hours for some of them, it was not until the end of the century that the concept of children working at all was questioned.

Unlike children higher up the social scale, the poor children of Victorian England did not enjoy a special period of childhood at all. They received no privileges or dispensations because of their age; many were not properly provided for, cared for or protected and very few received even a basic education. Some poor children were forced to take on adult roles and responsibilities at a very young age and some were entirely alone and had to provide and fend for themselves. With no legislation, agencies or state machinery to protect them, poor children were at the mercy of parents, employers and other adults with the result that many were abandoned, neglected, exploited and cruelly treated. In the eyes of the law children were the property of their parents and had no rights of their own. For much of the century there was very little concern in most quarters about the suffering of such children. Victorian sentimentality about childhood was reserved for children higher up the social scale.

Victorian London and its inhabitants were a source of much contemporary interest and were popular subjects for journalists, writers, diarists, artists and photographers, who all played an important part in drawing attention to the plight of the metropolitan poor. A considerable amount of the contemporary evidence about Victorian London has survived and provides a fascinating insight into the city in general and the London poor in particular. It is from this evidence that much of the story of the street children of Victorian London has been drawn.

THE EARLIER VICTORIAN PERIOD

1837–1870

CHAPTER 1

Setting the Scene

It is night. Calm and unmoved amidst the scenes that darkness favours, the great heart of London throbs in its Giant breast. Wealth and beggary, vice and virtue, guilt and innocence, repletion and the direst hunger, all treading on each other and crowding together, are gathered around it ... Does not this Heart of London, that nothing moves, nor stops, nor quickens – that goes on the same let what will be done – does it not express the City's character well?

Charles Dickens
Master Humphrey's Clock, 1841

Contemporary historical sources reveal four significant factors about early to mid-Victorian London. These were its vast size, its varying and contrasting scenes, its great attraction or pull factor, and its desperate need of modernisation.

In 1844 Friedrich Engels, a German socialist and co-author of *The Communist Manifesto*, wrote the following account of the profound impression which the sight of the Victorian metropolis had on him:

I know nothing more imposing than the view which the Thames offers during the ascent from the sea to London Bridge. The masses of buildings, the wharves on both shores, especially from Woolwich upwards, the countless ships along both shores, crowding ever closer and closer together, until, at last, only a narrow passage remains in the middle of the river, a passage through which hundreds of steamers shoot by one another; all this is so vast, so impressive, that a man cannot collect himself, but is lost in the marvel of England's greatness before he sets foot upon English soil.[1]

London was equally impressive from other angles. In 1861 Henry Mayhew, a novelist and journalist, went up in a hot-air balloon to survey the capital from above. It seemed to him like a mighty sea monster, which he named 'the leviathan metropolis'. London was so vast that:

it was impossible to see where the monster city began or ended, for the buildings stretched not only to the horizon on either side, but far away into the distance, where, owing to the coming shades of evening and the dense fumes from the million chimneys, the town seemed to blend into the sky, so that there was no distinguishing earth from heaven.[2]

Mayhew saw London as 'a world of its own', with Belgravia and Bethnal Green as the two poles (so different were they), with Temple Bar as the equator and the spreading suburbs resembling great continents. London was, indeed, like a voracious monster in the way it sprawled, consuming the surrounding countryside in the process.

London was the capital of the world's first industrial and richest nation. It was the business, financial and commercial capital through whose port Britain traded with all parts of the globe. It was also an important manufacturing centre; its industries included shipbuilding, tanning, brewing and clothes, furniture, brick and precision instrument making. London was a place of constant activity whose population rose with unprecedented speed during the nineteenth century. In 1800 its population was 1 million; by 1900 this had increased to 4.5 million. This incredible population rise was due to natural increase and immigration from other parts of Britain, especially the countryside, and from abroad.

Part of the great fascination of early to mid-nineteenth century London was its many changing faces and contrasting scenes. The metropolis represented different things to different people and provided a wide range of experiences. Anyone travelling across it from north to south or east to west would have encountered a huge variety of scenes. London also changed from hour to hour. The great contrasts within the metropolis included old London, evident, for example, in the remains of the old medieval city and its ancient churches, and new London, to be found in such places as the modernised West End and the railway termini.

The ugly parts of London, such as the slums, contrasted with the splendour of buildings like St Paul's Cathedral, Westminster Abbey and the grand residential squares. Working London was to be found in the City, the docklands and industrial areas, while London at leisure was to be found in the parks, theatres, opera houses and tourist spots. The constant bustle, noise and vibrancy of the streets and markets contrasted with the silence and sombre atmosphere of the capital's graveyards.

The City, the West End and the East End were all quite different places with their own distinct characteristics and atmosphere. The City was changing from a busy centre of trade, small industry, shopkeepers and a large residential area into a financial centre of offices, banks and insurance companies. It was in the process of becoming the financial centre of the world. The West End was the wealthiest, and arguably the most attractive, face of London. This area of splendid residential squares and expensive shops was busy during the 'season' but quiet for the rest of the year. The East End was very different as it was still a seafaring district at the beginning of the Victorian era. Its main industries were ship-building and its associated trades, and silk-weaving. Many of its residents were dockworkers living in jerry-built houses. By mid-century the East End was changing; its old industries had declined and 'noxious' trades such as glue and soap-making, formerly located in the City, moved in. The area also became a magnet for the poorest residents of the City who were displaced by its transformation into a financial centre.

One of the greatest contrasts was between London by day and London by night. During the day the streets were colourful, crowded, hectic and noisy. As night approached, on the other hand, the colours faded and the gas-lights came on, making the capital shadowy, sinister and threatening. It was even inhabited by different people.

People came to London for a variety of reasons. It had always been attractive as the capital city – the place where things were happening. Many had been lured to London over the centuries to seek their fortunes. This pull factor drew large numbers of people to the metropolis after the Industrial Revolution, including redundant agricultural workers looking for work. It continued to operate throughout the Victorian period. In the 1850s a million desperate Irish people came to London, driven by poverty and hunger following the potato famine of 1848–9. The capital seemed to draw people down on their luck. Attracted by its huge casual labour market, they sought work in the industrial areas, in the docks, on building sites, in railway construction, in markets and on the streets. Most, unfortunately, soon discovered that London did not live up to their expectations and found themselves struggling to survive among the destitute and homeless.

The metropolis was also a place of great fascination and interest to tourists and day visitors. They came to see for themselves the capital of the world's greatest nation. Some came from the continent and others arrived on steamships from more distant countries – especially America. The new railways made travel simpler, cheaper and speedier than it had previously been. A plethora of handbooks, visitor guides and pocket street-atlases were published at this time, testimony to the huge number of visitors. A vast array of attractions were on offer in the capital. Some sights, such as the Tower of London and St Paul's Cathedral, were old; others were newer, including Buckingham Palace and the rebuilt Houses of Parliament. The latest, distinctively Victorian, attractions included London Zoo, Wyld's Monster Globe in Leicester Square and the Polytechnic in Regent Street – an educational and entertainment venue. There were also plenty of open spaces, such as Hyde Park and Kensington Gardens with their bandstands and lakes. Visitors included the English upper classes, who came annually during the parliamentary session for 'the season'. While their men-folk were otherwise engaged, the women enjoyed London's attractions and the social whirl.

In May 1851 6 million people flocked to the capital, from home and abroad, to see the Great Exhibition, of which Prince Albert was a leading organiser. It was held in Joseph Paxton's amazing iron and glass 'Crystal Palace' in Hyde Park. The exhibition displayed items from around the globe but was really intended to show off Britain's manufactured goods and her industrial prowess. The exhibition, which symbolised London's position in the world and its growing importance as an imperial capital, remained open for nearly six months.

The other significant factor about the metropolis at this time was its desperate need of modernisation. Improvements were essential to transform London for its role as the centre of an expanding empire but, above all, changes had to be made to accommodate the unprecedented rise in its population. The existing housing stock and infrastructure simply could not cope under the pressure of mass immigration. Those members of the poorest classes who had some sort of roof over their heads were housed in slums across the metropolis. They lived in appallingly overcrowded, dilapidated, insanitary and disease-ridden tenements and jerry-built houses. There was an increasing need for these blots on the metropolitan landscape to be removed and alternative housing provided for the poor.

The capital's roads were narrow, congested and dangerous; road accidents and traffic jams were daily occurrences. Many roads were unmade and full of pot-holes. All London's roads were filthy with coal dust and animal dung. A lot of pavements were dusty or muddy, depending on the weather, as only parts of the capital were properly paved. Pavements were as congested as the roads and there was a pressing need for cheap public transport to relieve them. Guidebooks advised pedestrians not to stop on London pavements because of the risk of being kicked or pushed.

Another obstacle to progress on the London streets was cattle being driven to the livestock market at Smithfield, adding to the dirt and squalor. Inadequate street lighting, with a few areas still lit by smelly, smoking oil-lamps, was another inconvenience. The notorious London smogs, a mixture of chimney smoke, fog and fumes from the contaminated Thames, were yet another nuisance and health hazard. The Thames, another part of the transport infrastructure, was also crowded and congested.

Probably the most acute problem in early to mid-Victorian London, however, was the lack of clean drinking water and a proper, safe sewage system. Two thousand open sewers, and much of London's municipal and industrial waste, were emptied into the Thames and its tributary the Fleet. The former supplied half of the capital's drinking water. In the slum districts sewage ran down open gutters in the streets. Unsurprisingly, London was named the 'capital of cholera' and the *Lancet* described it as 'a doomed city'. The metropolis suffered repeated outbreaks of cholera, typhus and other water-borne diseases, resulting in a high mortality rate, especially among the young.

Not only were there too many living people for London's infrastructure and public services to cope with but there were also too many dead people. London was bursting at the seams both above and below ground. The long established graveyards and the eight private cemeteries built around the capital in the 1830s no longer had enough space in which to bury all the dead. Burials were piled on top of each other and were perilously close to the surface, causing an appalling smell which spread to nearby streets. This was another serious health hazard in urgent need of addressing.

Yet another major problem in London at this time was crime. The rapid increase in population, the high level of unemployment and the inability of the Poor Law to deal with all those in need led to a crime explosion. The Metropolitan Police, which had been founded in 1829 by Robert Peel, was a vast improvement on the old parish constables, Bow Street Runners and night watchmen. It was an efficient and professional force of uniformed officers, detectives and river police. The visible presence of constables on the beat and stationed at certain points throughout the metropolis was a deterrent to some extent. The Metropolitan Police did their best to cope with the ever-rising tide of crime as well as helping tourists and other visitors. The City of London maintained its own separate force. Old prisons needed to be modernised and new prisons needed to be built to accommodate the ever-expanding criminal population. The penal system itself also needed to be reformed.

A huge stumbling block to reform in early to mid-Victorian London was that responsibility for the capital's infrastructure and public services was divided between a multitude of local parishes, bodies and companies with often conflicting concerns and interests. To complicate matters further, the City of London was self-governing and largely autonomous. All this resulted in confusion, disagreement, delay and inaction when decisiveness, action and reform were urgently needed. The improvement and modernisation of Victorian London was a gradual process. Some problems were being addressed by mid-century but it took much longer for others to be remedied. The housing problem fell into the latter category. Slum clearance began during this period as part of the improvement process but instead of the very poor benefiting from this, it made their predicament worse. Some of the earliest clearance was carried out in the old City, where slum homes began to be demolished to make way for offices and commercial buildings. Thousands of the very poor were displaced as a result but no provision was made for re-housing them. Consequently, the slum dwellers of the city became more and more densely packed into the remaining slums. This happened across the metropolis to allow for the construction of new roads, railways and buildings.

Public health and sanitation increasingly became matters for concern and debate during the 1840s. They were highlighted in a number of publications, of which the most important was *An Inquiry into the Sanitary Conditions of the Labouring Population of Great Britain* by Edwin Chadwick, a Poor Law

Commissioner, published in 1842. He drew attention to the link between filthy, overcrowded living conditions and infectious diseases and concluded that poverty was the result of environment and not the moral failings of the poor. This conclusion flew in the face of prevailing assumptions. Growing concerns, and fears that disease-carrying air might waft from the slums to better areas, led to the Public Health and Sewers Act of 1848. This established a General Board of Health in London and appointed a Medical Officer of Health to investigate the issue of infectious disease.

It took a long time for the public health problems of London to be resolved, however, due to feuds between vested interests and a failure to understand that water carried disease. Matters came to a head in 1858, the year of 'The Great Stink', when a combination of the offensive smell of the Thames and a period of hot weather began to affect proceedings in the Houses of Parliament. All obstacles to reform were finally removed and Joseph Bazalgette, an engineer employed by the recently created Metropolitan Board of Works, was commissioned to design and build a proper, safe sewage system. This was completed by the late 1860s and effectively ended the regular outbreaks of cholera and other water-borne diseases and greatly improved the health of Londoners. Sanitary conditions were also improved by the Metropolitan Burials Act of 1852, under which new public cemeteries were built and Parish Burial Boards were established to ensure safe burial practice.

The establishment of the Metropolitan Board of Works in 1855 was important because it was the first unified body with responsibility for London's infrastructure and public services. In addition to sewerage and drainage, it became responsible for street improvements, bye-laws and building regulations. Road widening, straightening and building began in the 1840s and continued throughout this period. Important new roads included New Oxford Street, Farringdon Street and Southwark Street. The removal of road and bridge tolls also eased traffic hold-ups. Obstructions caused by cattle on the streets ended with the construction of a new market in Copenhagen Fields, Islington, in 1855. Additional bridges were built across the Thames to take pressure off London and Westminster bridges, two notorious bottlenecks. The embankment of the river was also started at this time, taking traffic away from Fleet Street and the Strand, ending flooding and replacing the muddy banks and ancient stairways down to the water. The new embankments changed the Thames from a wide and slow river to a narrower and faster-moving one. Some of the old docks were also demolished and replaced to increase the volume of river traffic.

Street congestion was eased considerably by the novel idea, proposed by the Surveyor to the City of London, of an underground railway. Despite initial fears and objections, the first line was opened in 1863 between Paddington and the City. Further lines were gradually added to complete the world's first underground railway system. This offered a quick and cheap alternative to omnibuses, cabs and other horse-drawn vehicles.

By this time many new railway lines had been laid above ground to connect London with the provinces. New mainline termini, including Waterloo, Paddington and Fenchurch Street, were built together with grand hotels to accommodate passengers. Local and suburban lines were also constructed which, along with the omnibuses, enabled workers who could afford the fares to live in the expanding suburbs and commute in to the centre to work.

A number of public buildings were constructed or re-built in the capital at this time. The most important were the Houses of Parliament, which were rebuilt following a fire in 1834 and finally completed in 1860. Other new buildings included the Public Record Office and the Foreign and Commonwealth Offices in Whitehall. In the 1860s the South Kensington museums, the Albert Hall and Memorial and the Imperial Institute were built with the profits of the Great Exhibition. Many of these public buildings were in the grand Gothic, Italianate and classical styles of architecture, befitting the world's richest city and the capital of a growing empire. More churches were built during this period for the expanding population, including the Metropolitan Tabernacle in South London, home of the great revivalist preacher Charles Haddon Spurgeon. New prisons included Pentonville, a model prison built to the new panoptican design, Wandsworth and Holloway. Among a number of new hospitals built in the capital were King's College and the Hospital for Sick Children in Great Ormond Street. This spate of building work made a considerable impact on the metropolitan landscape.

However, despite all the efforts to modernise, reform and improve London between 1837 and 1870 there was still a long way to go. It was against this background of an evolving city that another story was unfolding; a story that was by turns fascinating, tragic and uplifting but also one that brought shame on the capital of the Earth's richest nation. This was the story of the street children of Victorian London.

CHAPTER 2

The Early Social Investigative Journalists and Writers

My earnest hope is that the book may serve to give the rich a more intimate knowledge of the sufferings, and the frequent heroism under those sufferings, of the poor – that it may teach those who are beyond temptation to look with charity on the frailties of their less fortunate brethren ...

Henry Mayhew
Preface to *London Labour and the London Poor*, 1851

Reading was a popular pastime of the Victorian middle class. This period saw a huge increase in the publication of newspapers, magazines and periodicals. Improved literacy as the century progressed increased the demand for cheap literature. Daily papers at this time included the *Daily Telegraph*, the *Daily News*, *The Morning Chronicle* and the *Morning Post*. Weekly and Sunday papers were also available throughout the country. There were more than a hundred papers in the London suburbs alone.[1] Popular periodicals and magazines included *Cornhill*, *Punch, Household Words*, the *Pall Mall Gazette* and the *Illustrated London News*.

From the early years of Victoria's reign attention was drawn in the press to the plight of the urban poor and the widening gulf between social classes. The London poor often featured in books about the city in all its guises, a long established literary genre. Around this time the first examples of a new type of literature also appeared, much of which has survived and provides a rich source of information about the lives of the poor, especially in London. Certain members of the middle class, particularly journalists and clergymen, set out to explore, and report on, the homes, work and lives of the lowest classes. Some of these early social investigators, using the language and imagery of exploration, portrayed the London underclass as strange creatures who inhabited a different, undiscovered country which they had set out to explore and report back on. This curiosity about the poor may have been due to what Charles Dickens often referred to as 'the attraction of repulsion' for the 'low life' of the metropolis. It was this which drew

Dickens himself to the seedy areas of the city. A few foreign visitors also wrote about London's poorest citizens, which provided an interesting outsider's view. The results of these investigations were published in the press, magazines and books, often under pseudonyms or pen names.

The social investigators of this period were not only motivated by the need to sell newspapers and books but also by concern for the vast underclass at the bottom of the social pyramid. These victims of rapid industrialisation and social change could be seen on many of the streets and in all the slum districts of the capital. The social investigative writers asked searching questions about the poor, often addressed directly at the reader, and put forward suggestions for remedies and reform. As well as enlightening their readers, they spoke up for the poor and illiterate who had no voice of their own and highlighted the deficiencies of the government and those in authority. They stirred the moral consciences of the middle class, heightened their existing fears about the urban underclass, brought the subject of poverty into the open and influenced public opinion. The street children who belonged to this underclass became a particular focus of middle-class anxiety.

The revelations about the poor of early Victorian London appeared at a time when the 'condition of England' was in the forefront of people's minds and fears of social unrest had been unleashed by Chartist demonstrations. Although the better-off classes were aware of the plight of the poor from 'social novels' and reports of government inquiries, it was the social investigative writers who first opened their eyes to the true depth of poverty in the metropolis. The graphic descriptions of the suffering and struggles of real people, often expressed in alarming language, which began to appear in the press shocked readers. Many refused to accept the truth of the accounts. Nevertheless, judging by the enormous number of words written on the subject, a huge market developed for writing about the London poor. This rich historical source has been used to put together the story of the street children of early Victorian London. As this material is so extensive, only those writers used will be looked at in detail here.

Although modern readers are less familiar with his journalism than his novels, Charles Dickens was one of the best, most widely read and influential of the Victorian journalists. He started by writing articles and essays for newspapers and magazines such as the *Evening Chronicle* and *Bell's Life in London,* using the pseudonyms Boz and Tibbs. Some of his work was illustrated by George Cruikshank. London was Dickens's inspiration and fascinated him from childhood to the end of his life. 'What an inexhaustible food for speculation do the streets of London afford',[2] he exclaimed in an article written at the age of twenty-four. Dickens's extensive and intimate knowledge of London had been acquired when he was left to fend for himself at the age of twelve on his father's incarceration in a debtor's prison. At this lonely time the young boy took to wandering around the streets at all hours of the day and night. He became captivated by the sights, sounds and atmosphere of the metropolis and was particularly drawn to its slum districts. Above all, he was fascinated by the great variety of people who lived and worked in London.

Dickens's early journalism dealt with social problems and included reports of visits he made to the dark and grim places of Victorian London, including prisons, workhouses and the haunts of dangerous criminals. He became very concerned about the poor people he met and was able to empathise with them because of his own experience of poverty. He worried especially about children fending for themselves on the streets and was one of the first journalists to draw attention to their plight. Dickens knew what it was like to be cold, hungry, frightened and alone in the great city and acknowledged that if his family's circumstances had not improved he could well have become a street urchin himself.

In 1850 Dickens founded *Household Words* in which to publish his novels and 'to inform and instruct' his readers. This magazine was used to express his views on social issues, to campaign against injustices and to draw attention to the plight of London's poor and needy, including the street children. Dickens favoured the improvement of society rather than radical reform and defined the purpose of his social journalism as the 'raising up of those that are down and the general improvement of our social condition'.[3] He advocated improving the education of the poor to help them out of their poverty and improving the Poor Law. His aim was to fight oppression and dispel ignorance about the poor and their struggle to survive in the harsh urban environment of Victorian London. Dickens stirred the emotions and awakened the consciences of his readers. He did not express any political opinions but made clear his anger at government inaction and his contempt for people in a position of power who failed to help those in need. *Household Words* attracted a vast readership and sold up to 40,000 copies a week.

In 1859 Dickens started a new magazine called *All the Year Round* in which he published articles under the pseudonym of 'An Uncommercial Traveller' and adopted the persona of an inquisitive traveller in London. He always took the stance of a detached observer in his social journalism. It therefore lacked the immediacy which direct engagement with the people he wrote about would have created. Dickens rarely spoke directly to the poor himself but he did speak to and record the words of officials such as police inspectors and workhouse masters. Dickens's eye for eccentric characters and his powerful imagination were given free rein in his journalism.

Henry Mayhew also had a wide knowledge and curiosity about London and its people. He undertook his first social investigative journey in 1848 when he accompanied a doctor on a tour of Bermondsey during a cholera epidemic. His findings, which were published in *The Morning Chronicle*, helped to raise awareness of the desperate need for public health reform in London. Soon afterwards, the editor of *The Morning Chronicle* agreed to a suggestion from Mayhew for a series of investigative articles on the labouring classes of England

and Wales. Mayhew was given the task of investigating London with the help of a team of journalists; he became known to his readers as 'The Metropolitan Commissioner'. Mayhew's reports, in which he described himself as 'the traveller in the undiscovered country of the poor,'[4] were published in the form of seventy-six letters to the newspaper.

Mayhew's investigation took him all over the metropolis, to the streets, docks, market-places, sweat-shops, slums, prisons and workhouses. The focus of his inquiry was the poor people themselves and his direct engagement with them, which was the key to his success, resulted in something unique – the first attempt to tell the story of the poor in their own words. Mayhew crossed the barrier between his class and that of the people he interviewed so successfully that he referred to them as 'our street folk'.

The street folk included a large number of children. Mayhew wrote harrowing descriptions of the daily lives and struggles of these children and added numerical estimates of them drawn from official statistics. His vivid pictures, including details of their appearance, expressions, demeanour and mood, provide an unrivalled vein of information about the street children. Their stories, related in their own words and dialect, helped to bring them to life as real, suffering people.

Mayhew was not overtly political in his articles but made clear his opposition to free trade, which he considered a disadvantage to workers, exploitation of the poor and the government's 'laissez faire' policy towards them. He also questioned the prevailing belief that the poor were responsible for their own predicament and the argument that there was always enough work for those who sought it. Mayhew wanted to stir those 'in high places' to take action to improve the condition of those 'whose misery, ignorance and vice, amidst all the immense wealth and great knowledge of the first city in the world, is, to say the very least, a national disgrace to us'.[5] Mayhew, like many people of his class, was a great believer in self-help and favoured helping the poor to help themselves. He emphasised how many were doing their best to observe this middle-class tenet.

The *Morning Chronicle* articles about London provoked an astonishing response of shock and disbelief; they had a much greater impact than the reports of the provincial investigators. A correspondence began in the paper between Mayhew and concerned readers and donations poured in to help the people he had written about. In 1852, after falling out with the editor of *The Morning Chronicle,* Mayhew started to publish his articles himself in two-penny parts. His work was eventually published in the illustrated book *London Labour and the London Poor.* Further investigations by Mayhew in the 1850s formed the basis of his book *The Great World of London,* part of which became *The Criminals Prisons of London* (1862). This work, in which he was assisted by John Binny, provides a good source of material on criminal children and young prostitutes.

James Greenwood, who wrote for the *Pall Mall Gazette* and the *Daily Telegraph,* was one of a number of journalists who were influenced by Henry Mayhew. He was famous for disguising himself as a vagrant to get an insight into life in the casual ward of Lambeth Workhouse and wrote about the experience in an article entitled 'A Night in the Workhouse' (1866). Thereafter, he used 'The Amateur Casual' as his pen name. Greenwood's book *The Seven Curses of London* (1869) is a valuable source of information on the street children. His other works included *Sentimental Journeys or Highways of the Modern Babylon* (1867). Greenwood's aim was to enlighten his readers and help to change the lives of the poor. Despite his sympathy for the poor, however, Greenwood did not become close to them in the same way as Henry Mayhew did.

Another early social investigative writer was George Godwin, a surveyor and architect. He was editor of *The Builder,* an architectural journal concerned with social issues such as sanitary reform. Godwin's investigative focus was on the living conditions of the London poor. His illustrated book *London Shadows – A Glance at the 'Homes' of the Thousands* (1854) provides vivid and detailed descriptions of the slum homes which some of the street children lived in.

A similarly useful source on the slums of London in the earlier period is the writing of John Hollingshead. He was one of 'Dickens's Young Men', having worked for him on *Household Words* in the 1850s. He shared Dickens's fascination for and intimate knowledge of London and its people. In the severe winter of 1860–1, the worst of the century, Hollingshead was asked by the editor of the *Morning Post* to investigate the effect of the appalling weather on the London poor. Hollingshead set out on a thorough house-to-house investigation and reported his findings in a series of articles named *London Horrors.* In his detailed and graphic picture of the interior of slum homes and the domestic lives of the poor, Hollingshead noted a 'dead level of misery, crime, vice, dirt and rags' and a 'terrible sameness'[6] in the stories of the poor all over London. He described this as 'a glaring national disgrace' which Parliament 'babbles'[7] over occasionally but failed to deal with. His suggested remedies included self-help, education and Poor Law reform. Hollingshead's articles were later published as a book named *Ragged London in 1861.* He also wrote *London Underground* (1862), based on a survey of the capital's sewage workers. Other journalists and writers who have been used to a lesser extent as sources for the lives of the early street children include James Grant and Blanchard Jerrold.

The clergy with pastoral responsibility for the poor had been visiting the slums of London long before any social investigators set foot in them. Some clergymen added their voices to those of the journalists by publishing accounts of their experiences. The view of the Church was that each person's place in society was decreed by God but that Christians had a duty to help the lower classes by moral instruction and practical help. Clerical authors included Thomas Archer who wrote *The Pauper, the Thief and The Convict* (1865) and *The Terrible Sights of London* (1870), both of which provide valuable material on the street children.

A few foreign visitors to early Victorian London came expressly to study the poor and publish their findings. Two of these authors are used as sources for this book but because their works were not published in English at the time, they did not have any impact on the English public. Flora Tristan, a French socialist and feminist, recorded the findings of her visit to London in 1839 in *Promenades de Londres* (1842). Her purpose was to enlighten the French on the appalling predicament of the London poor whom she saw as victims of the English capitalist system. Friedrich Engels, the German socialist and co-author of *The Communist Manifesto,* published his observations and opinions on London poverty in *The Condition of the Working Class in England* (1845). With a political axe to grind, Engels also saw this poverty in terms of the poor struggling against middle-class oppression. He was particularly scathing about the English government, whose only action on behalf of the poor was to pay for a few commissions of inquiry, the reports of which were left to gather dust on a Home Office shelf. Other foreign visitors wrote for the tourist market and are a good source of information on the background to the lives of the street children.

The final primary source used as evidence for the lives of the London street children of this period is the diary of Arthur Munby, a lawyer and poet, who had a prurient interest in and fetish for working-class females engaged in rough and dirty physical work. His diary is a vivid, colourful and readable record of life in the Victorian metropolis.

CHAPTER 3

Who Were the Street Children?

Many of them are quite homeless; many of them are entirely neglected by their parents; many are orphans, outcasts, street beggars, crossing sweepers, and little hawkers of things about the streets; they are generally very ignorant, although in some points very quick and cunning.

William Locke, 1852
(Secretary to the London Ragged School Union)

It is difficult to state precisely how many children lived, or spent most of their lives, on the streets of early to mid-Victorian London. Contemporary opinion was divided on this issue; James Greenwood and Thomas Archer estimated that they numbered 100,000 whereas Lord Shaftesbury and Henry Mayhew made a much more conservative estimate of 30,000. The true number was most likely to have been between these two figures. Most contemporary commentators, however, would have agreed with Mayhew's definition of a child as being under the age of fifteen, when the adult characteristics, or 'ruling passion', had been formed.

The majority of the street children were boys and they came from a variety of backgrounds. Some were indigenous Londoners and some came from other parts of Britain, particularly Ireland following the famine of 1848–9, and from the English countryside. They had arrived in London, with their families or alone, in search of work. Others were the children of foreigners, including Italian and Jewish settlers.

The street children can be divided into those with some sort of family support and those without. The first category included those from families so poor that they could not survive without the few pennies which even the youngest child could earn and their children were forced onto the streets to work, beg or obtain money by whatever means they could. Young widows and deserted mothers were often compelled to rely on their children's help in this way.

Some children were on the streets because both parents worked long hours to support their families and were, therefore, unable to look after them. Countless children were to be seen playing or wandering unsupervised at all hours in the slum districts. The smallest children were often looked after by older ones, usually siblings or a young neighbour entrusted with their care for a few pennies a day. The children who played in the gutters in Drury Lane Court, near the Strand, for example, were mostly the offspring of workers in Covent Garden Market or those who hung around there on the look-out for work.

Children without family support included those who had come to London alone in search of work and ended up struggling to survive on the streets, and those who were simply enticed by the freedom and independence of street life. Also in this category were children who had run away from their homes and families, often due to mistreatment by brutal parents and step-parents. Mayhew noted that the very poor often took out 'their annoyances or disappointments ... in passionate beating and cursing their children for trifling or for no causes'.[1] This was because they had 'fewer conventional restraints'[2] than the higher social classes. Cruelty and miserable home lives were frequently caused by drunkenness, which was the only way many members of the underclass could cope with the appalling hardships they had to endure. Some children were on the streets because they had been neglected by parents so drunken and feckless that they were incapable of shouldering their responsibilities. This group also included former child apprentices and servants who had fled from harsh masters and mistresses. Life for these runaways must have been truly unbearable if living on the streets seemed an attractive alternative.

Children from struggling working-class homes who had been pushed out to fend for themselves, usually by the arrival of another baby, also came into this category. Such an occurrence often meant that there was no longer enough space in a crowded home or enough money to feed another child. The result was that an older child had to leave and support him or herself. Such children were described by the poor as having been sent out to 'cut their own grass' or to 'fish for themselves'.

Orphans and abandoned children also formed part of this group. Some orphans were fortunate enough to be taken in and cared for by relatives, friends or kindly neighbours. Many, however, had nowhere to go but the streets. To obtain a place in an orphanage, a child generally needed to be recommended by a subscriber or patron. The poorest children were unlikely to have known anyone able to recommend them. Abandoned children included those left with the notorious baby-farmers who advertised in the cheap newspapers. Desperate mothers, usually unmarried and alone, risked using them because they could not work and care for a baby at the same time. Some infants entrusted to baby-farmers were dumped on the streets. Other poor infants were handed over to 'adopters' for around £12. Once the money was paid there was nothing to stop these children being abandoned anywhere in London. Although a few strays found their way into good homes, the majority ended up in the poorest districts, often in brothels or among criminals. Even the worst characters would not leave a small child to starve if they could help it. Once these children had reached an age when they could earn some money they were invariably cast out to fend for themselves. Most of the neglected children who became thieves were originally abandoned by bogus child-adopters.

There was a contemporary stereotype of the London street child which they did not all, by any means, fit. This stereotype, and the general attitude towards the street children, is illustrated by the derogatory names commonly used to depict them. These included 'street arabs', 'guttersnipes', 'wild or monkey tribes', 'ruffians', 'ragamuffins' and 'hottentots'. Street children were described as 'roaming' or 'swarming' in 'armies' and 'hordes'. These derogatory names were even used by people who sympathised with the street children. The impression conveyed was of thousands of filthy, ragged, abusive, feral savages running amok in the capital.

An article published in *Punch* magazine in 1842 perfectly illustrated the way in which the street children were regarded. They were depicted as cunning, disrespectful nuisances who plagued and abused anyone unfortunate enough to cross their paths. They were said to fear no-one in authority except the police and it was claimed that their leading characteristic was 'a singular antipathy to work of any description'.[3] The street children were also patronisingly portrayed as comic figures and objects of fun in *Punch* cartoons. This stereotype was unjust because a significant number of these children did not fit it. It was Lord Shaftesbury who first drew attention to the large number of street children in early Victorian London in an article in the *Quarterly Review* in 1845. Shaftesbury was very sympathetic towards them but even he appeared to have a stereotypical image of the street child.

Many, probably the majority, of the street children had received no care, affection, discipline, restraint, moral, spiritual or other guidance from adults. Other, more fortunate, children had received early care and guidance from adults who had tried to do their best for them. Some who had benefited from such lessons had forgotten them once on the streets and exposed to the temptations, risks and dangers of London and the bad influence of other children.

The street children can be divided into two categories. This is only a rough division because some children had a mixture of characteristics common to both categories and did not fit neatly into either. The first was mainly made up of boys and comprised those who enjoyed the freedom and lack of adult control which their vagrant lives allowed. They appeared not to suffer greatly from the hardships of life on the streets and were resilient, self-reliant, tough, street-wise, wild, cunning, insubordinate and precocious. Lord Shaftesbury described these children as enjoying 'a barbarian freedom from all restraint'.[4]

Children in this category had a habit of acquiring enough money to eat, drink and enjoy themselves for a while until their money ran out and they were compelled to get hold of some more. They survived mainly by selling, begging and stealing and often presented a happy, carefree persona which may have been a brave face put on to cover underlying vulnerability, anxiety and distress. These children mainly, but not exclusively, fitted the feral stereotype of the street-child. The negative characteristics they displayed and their bad behaviour, which included swearing, drinking and gambling, alarmed middle-class London. These children were the very opposite of clean, godly, meek, innocent, respectful, compliant, obedient and well-brought up middle-class children. Feral street-children posed such a threat because they turned the natural order of the middle-class world upside down. They directly challenged adult authority and were a threat to a well-ordered society[5] in which children and the lower classes had a divinely ordained place. Henry Mayhew summed up the background of this type of street child as follows:

> Parental instruction; the comforts of a home, however humble – the great moral truths upon which society itself rests:- the influence of proper example; the power of education; the effect of useful amusement; are all denied to them, or come to them so greatly vitiated, that they rather tend to increase, than to repress, the very evils they were intended to remedy.[6]

In the second category were children who were much closer to the middle-class ideal. These children, both boys and girls, were generally honest, law-abiding, hard-working, meek, respectful, polite and articulate. They worked long hours to support themselves or to contribute to their family's income. Their lives were tough and relentless with little or no time for enjoyment. Some in this group, overwhelmed by the struggle to survive, were weak, pale, puny, sickly and depressed. Others were stronger and more resilient, like the children in the other category.

Mayhew recorded several other interesting facts about the street children in general. He noticed how ignorant many of them were; even those who had received some education seemed to know little or nothing about the world around them or even about the city in which they lived. They knew next to nothing about the Bible and, as a rule, did not attend church. Most knew only what was necessary for survival, such as basic money skills and the cost of goods in the wholesale markets, and had no opinions on anything which did not directly affect their daily lives. Mayhew also noticed how selfish many street children were. He put this down to the hard struggles they had to endure and the lack of sympathy they received in the process. Also, although there was companionship among them there was little evidence of true friendship. Another fact Mayhew recorded was that street children tended to enter puberty early and possessed what he described as an 'extreme animal fondness for the opposite sex'.[7]

The derogatory language used to describe the street-children revealed the long-established unease of the middle class concerning their social inferiors. A lingering fear had existed since the disturbances of the city mob in eighteenth-century London, and then the French Revolution, that the poor may become dissatisfied with their lot and rise up against those above them in the social pyramid. This fear had recently been reignited by revolutions in a number of continental cities in 1848. The street-children were already a visible threat in London and their portrayal in such negative and inflammatory language in the press and other literature added to the fears and disquiet of their social superiors.

CHAPTER 4

Scratching a Living: Selling and Finding

The pavement and the road are crowded with purchasers and street-sellers ... Little boys, holding three or four onions in their hand, creep between the people, wriggling their way through every interstice, and asking for custom in whining tones, as if seeking charity.

Henry Mayhew
London Labour and the London Poor, 1851

... deep in the mud, stood the boys, clamouring for largess and prepared to dive down in the sluggish ooze, to fight with one another, to exhaust a whole vocabulary of abuse, for the smallest copper coin.

James Payn
Lights and Shadows of London Life, 1867

A vast number of street vendors plied their trade in early to mid-Victorian London. According to Henry Mayhew's estimation, the costermongers (sellers of fruit and vegetables) alone numbered 30,000 in 1851. A large proportion of these traders were children, some as young as six. Almost any item could be bought on the streets of the capital, including live animals and caged birds. It was claimed that at Whitechapel Market in the East End everything could be bought to 'furnish a house, feed a family and plant a garden'.[1] Vendors advertised their presence and their wares by street cries.

The population of the metropolis at this time, both native Londoners and immigrants, was swollen daily by office, shop and manual workers from the suburbs, as well as by day-trippers, tourists and shoppers. This cosmopolitan crowd, from all social classes, supplied a steady stream of customers for the street traders, who went wherever there was a profit to be made. Much of their custom came from people as poor as themselves who were not welcome in respectable shops and could only afford to buy small quantities at a time.

Street vendors worked in street markets; shopping areas such as the West End, Cheapside and The Strand; the commercial streets of the City; alleys; thoroughfares; public parks and gardens; tourist spots; amusement venues; and in residential areas, including the slums where many of them lived. Many had regular pitches on street corners, near theatres or outside public houses and some traded in the same areas every day. Others trudged the streets hawking their goods, often walking mile after mile in the hope of catching chance custom. There were also vendors who combined stationary selling with travelling to markets both inside and outside the metropolis.

Despite the plentiful supply of customers, this was a very hard way to earn a living. There was fierce competition from other vendors and the army of street traders was regularly swollen from the vast ranks of the unemployed. The enormous influx of visitors to London for the Great Exhibition of 1851 encouraged many more to have a go at making their living in this way. Having to keep a constant look-out for the police did not make the job any easier. The police, called 'bobbies' or 'crushers' by the poor, continually harassed and moved traders on.

Children of both sexes worked as street sellers in London. They included those sent out by their families as well as those who worked alone or in gangs for self-survival. Children mostly sold easy to carry items with small start-up costs such as matches, fly-papers, shoe and stay-laces, money bags, nuts, oranges, water-cresses and flowers. Another group of child street sellers were the children of costermongers, who were trained in the job by their parents from an early age. Many of these children, the majority of whom were Irish, went on to become costermongers in their own right when they were old enough.

The child street sellers worked long hours, during which they were exposed to the elements in inadequate clothing and often without shoes. Those selling fresh goods had to be at the wholesale markets at 4 a.m. when they opened to sell produce as it arrived from the market gardens around London. Covent Garden and Farringdon Markets supplied fruit, vegetables and flowers. Children selling flowers often made their way to the railway stations to catch the early commuters. Many child street workers could buy a meal, usually from one of the numerous ready-prepared food stalls, only when they had made enough to pay for it.

Some children walked miles every day to sell their wares, frequently working well into the evening to catch the late trade, especially around theatres and other amusement places. Sellers of nuts and oranges usually trudged around the public houses until they closed. At the end of a long, hard day, children sent out by their parents sometimes had only a few pennies to take home. Some risked a beating if their takings were small. To avoid this, children often stayed out all night until they had made enough money to return without fear. Children without a home slept in lodging houses, if they could afford to, in night shelters for the homeless, or rough on the streets.

Most child vendors worked weekends as well as weekdays. The weekend markets were more like fairs than markets with their bright lights and colourful stalls. New Cut Market off Waterloo Road and The Brill in Somers Town were two of the busiest. These markets provided an opportunity for the child vendors to make a bit more profit. Their main customers were the working classes who, having been paid for their week's work, went out to buy food. Not all the child sellers were honest; some used selling as a cover for begging, an offence under the Vagrancy Act of 1824, or for picking the pockets of unwary shoppers. Many children, like adult sellers, were also unscrupulous and routinely cheated customers with short weights and imperfect goods.

Henry Mayhew interviewed a number of child street sellers for his articles published in *The Morning Chronicle* in 1849 and uncovered some poignant stories. One was the story of the little water-cress girl. This illiterate eight-year-old lived in Clerkenwell with her mother and step-father, a cleaner and a scissor-grinder. She was not a stereotypical street child as she was honest, hard-working, polite, articulate and respectful. This is how Mayhew described her appearance:

> The poor child, although the weather was severe, was dressed in a thin cotton gown, with a threadbare shawl wrapped round her shoulders. She wore no covering to her head, and the long rusty hair stood out in all directions. When she walked she shuffled along, for fear that the large carpet slippers that served her for shoes should slip off her feet.[2]

This child's face was 'pale and thin with privation' and 'wrinkled where the dimples ought to have been'.[3]

This little girl worked all day selling 'creases' on the streets to earn 3*d* or 4*d* as her contribution to the family income. At weekends she did household chores for a Jewish family to earn a little extra money and her food. Her diet at home consisted of bread and butter and tea, with meat once a week. The little girl told Mayhew that she was treated well at home and, as evidence, cited the fact that her mother did not beat her often. However, she admitted that she was happiest when working for the 'kind' Jewish family, who had given her the few toys she possessed.

Mayhew immediately noticed how this young child had been forced by her family's circumstances to grow up prematurely. She had 'entirely lost all childish ways' and acquired the attitude and manners of an adult.

> There was something cruelly pathetic in hearing this infant, so young that her features had scarcely formed themselves, talking of the bitterest struggles of life, with the calm earnestness of one who had endured them all.[4]

This child's maturity was evident in her lack of self-pity and her matter-of-fact acceptance of her situation. Mayhew, viewing her from a middle-class perspective, was surprised at this. Like other members of his class, he knew that poor children were compelled to work but the sordid details shocked him. Many of his readers would have shared his shock.

The little water-cress girl was proud of her adult role and her responsibility as someone 'as has a living to earn'.[5] She was particularly proud of her ability at bargaining with the saleswomen in Farringdon Market from whom she bought her 'creases'. Nevertheless, she was clearly torn between the adult and child world. Her adult attitude contrasted with her pleasure in the toys she described to Mayhew and her excitement when he told her about the London parks 'with green grass and tall trees, where beautiful carriages drove about, and people walked for pleasure, and children played'.[6] Knowing only the streets where she lived and worked, this girl had no knowledge of the existence of such places. 'Would they let such as me go there – just to look?'[7] she asked in wonder. The little girl perceived immediately that she would be excluded from these parks both by her class and her lack of leisure time due to her premature ejection into the adult world of work. She was acutely aware of, and accepted her position among, the dregs of Victorian society. In a very mature way she showed no envy of the fortunate children who played in the parks or expressed any bitterness at her exclusion. She stated quite philosophically that there was 'no use'[8] in crying about her plight. Mayhew's response to this child's story was a mixture of shock, compassion and, above all, admiration at her stoicism, acceptance and complete lack of self-pity.

Another story told by Mayhew was that of the two orphan flower girls aged fifteen and eleven. Like the little water-cress girl, these children were far from the stereotypical feral street child, except in their appearance.

> Both were clad in old, but not torn, dark print frocks, hanging so closely, yet so loosely, about them as to show the deficiency of under-clothing; they wore old broken black chip bonnets. The older sister (or rather half-sister) had a pair of old worn out shoes on her feet, the younger was barefoot, but trotted along, in a gait at once quick and feeble – as if the soles of her little feet were impervious, like horn, to the roughness of the road.[9]

The older girl had 'pinched' features but the younger, surprisingly, was round, chubbier and healthier looking. Their late mother had worked as a chairwoman and during her lifetime they had enjoyed a comparatively good standard of living. The children had never known their fathers. They barely survived by selling flowers and oranges on a round of the London streets which stretched as far as St John's Wood, Highgate and Hampstead in North London.

Mayhew interviewed the sisters in the damp, sparsely furnished room in the slums off Drury Lane which they shared with their brother, their kindly landlady and her husband. Their joint earnings just covered their rent and a starvation diet of bread, tea and an occasional herring. The older sister, like the water-cress girl, had been propelled into an adult role at the age of seven by her mother's death. She had assumed responsibility for her younger siblings and supported them herself, without seeking help from the parish. They could all read and write as they had somehow managed to continue their education. They regularly attended Mass and, despite her terrible privations and sufferings, the older girl firmly believed that God would support them. She was clearly aware of the way the street children were regarded by society as she was anxious to show that she had been well brought up and made a point of saying 'I never go among boys.'[10]

The flower girls provide an example of children who were forced to work on the streets after falling down the social scale due to unfortunate circumstances beyond their control. Their resilience, determination in the face of adversity and lack of self pity were remarkable. These children were, nevertheless, better off than many in a similar position because of the kindness shown to them by their landlady. She had taken them with her whenever she moved home, did household chores for them and helped them when they needed stock-money, even pawning her own goods when necessary. The flower girls and their brother were also lucky in that they had each other, and in their good start in life. Mayhew did not comment on this story or betray his feelings, as he sometimes did when writing about the street children. He left his readers to come to their own conclusions.

Another heart-rending tale was that of an unnamed seller of small, inexpensive items, referred to as 'the Cheap John'. He was a young man when he told Mayhew about his life as a child street seller in London during the early years of Victoria's reign. This son of travelling sellers was neglected and mistreated from his earliest years because of his parents' drink problem. As a small child he was sent out each day with a roll of matches to sell and beaten if he did not make much money. As he explained to Mayhew:

> My father was an inveterate drinker and (had) a very violent temper. My mother, I am sorry to say, used to drink too, but I believe that ill-usage drove her to it. They had a dreadful life; I scarcely felt any attachment for them, home we had none, one place was as good as another to us.[11]

At the age of eight, this boy left home following a harsh beating with just 9*d* worth of matches to make his own way in the world. He travelled from Dover to London and survived by selling matches and song-sheets. He slept on the streets or in rough lodging houses when he could afford to. Occasionally he met kind people who helped him, including an old soldier who taught him how to read his song-sheets to improve his chances of selling them.

As frequently happened with the street children, he acquired bad habits from mixing with other children. He took to gambling and was often cheated out of all his money, resulting in 'great privations'.[12] No matter how desperate the Cheap

John was, however, he could not bring himself to beg. He had two spells in prison and had to endure punishment on the treadmill. On the first occasion he was arrested simply because a police constable objected to the phosphorous boxes he was selling; on the second occasion he was caught selling goods without a licence. During his time in prison, however, this boy turned down 'opportunities and offers of gratuitous instruction'[13] on becoming a thief. After each spell of imprisonment the Cheap John 'was thrust out upon the world heart-broken, without a shilling, to beg, to steal or to starve'.[14] Against the odds, he overcame numerous setbacks to become a licensed trader, to marry a shopkeeper and to earn enough to support a family. The Cheap John succeeded in moving up the social scale to become a member of the respectable, industrious working class.

This story shows how completely alone and friendless many of London's street children were. It also illustrates the overwhelming odds they faced and the sort of setbacks they had to overcome. After an appalling start in life, this boy had to contend with loneliness, a gambling addiction, the hostility of the police, unsympathetic magistrates and a harsh prison system, as well as the struggle to survive on the streets. As a child and a teenager the Cheap John surmounted difficulties many adults would have been unable to overcome. His experience begs the question of how many other children, faced with the same problems, gave up the struggle and ended up in a pauper's grave. There is no way of knowing how many other children in the same position did not survive.

None of these child sellers were stereotypical street children. All were polite, respectful, intelligent, articulate and worked hard to survive by honest means. The Cheap John came in contact with feral street children and during that time probably fell into that category.

Another way of scratching a living in London at this time was by finding and scavenging things to sell. Street finders and scavengers, both adults and children, included pure finders who collected dogs' mess to sell to the tanneries of Bermondsey, where it was used as a purifier in the leather-making process, and cigarette or 'hard-up' finders, who picked up cigarette ends to dry and sell to the poor. Others gathered rags and bones or worked as sewer scavengers, known as 'toshers'. Scavenging in the sewers became popular when work began on the construction of Joseph Bazalgette's new sewerage system.

One group of scavengers, the mudlarks, included a considerable number of children. Anyone approaching London by vessel along the Thames would have seen hordes of these desperate people on both sides of the river. They were there throughout the year, in all weathers, spread along the shoreline, barely communicating with each other as they intently raked the mudflats in search of anything worth selling. When the tide came in, the mudlarks were forced to leave the riverbanks. They then ventured into the nearby streets to sell their finds in the numerous rag shops and marine stores. Some mudlarks made the most of the time between tides by scraping the mud off their clothes and doing odd jobs on the streets, such as opening cab doors and holding horses, to earn extra money. Although they worked away from the main streets of London and largely kept to themselves, the young mudlarks sometimes came in contact with the other street children. Some young mudlarks lived in slum homes and lodging houses in the squalid alleys and courtyards near the river but many were homeless and forced to sleep on the streets.

Mayhew recorded a number of interesting facts about the child mudlarks. He discovered that the majority were boys as the girls who tried the job were nearly all enticed away by the easier and more lucrative occupation of prostitution. He also noted that most of these children were orphans or fatherless, with many compelled to work because their widowed mothers were too poor to keep them. The few with parents were often the children of coal-whippers or came from poor Irish families. Mayhew also noticed how ignorant the majority of child mudlarks were and how few had received even the most basic education.

The three main areas in which the mudlarks worked were around the Pool of London near Tower Bridge, in the vicinity of the yards where vessels were built and repaired, and around the coal wharves. Those who worked around the Pool carried baskets or tin kettles to hold their finds, or used their hats or caps for this purpose. Working six or seven hours at a stretch, in unimaginable conditions, these children searched for items such as coal, rope, driftwood, metal, copper nails, animal bones and bottles. Occasionally they were lucky enough to find a purse or a valuable object like a tool but most of their finds fetched only a few pennies. Coal, for example, was sold to the poor for 7*d* per 14 lb pot.

As long as the mudlarks kept to the mudflats they were left alone, but if they ventured near the wharves where the goods barges were moored they had to look out for the wharfingers (owners or caretakers of the barges). The punishment for being caught on one of these was seven days in a House of Correction. Nevertheless, the valuable items on the barges were a great temptation to the young mudlarks, if they could get near them. The more daring ones sometimes got onto the barges and threw goods to their comrades, or into the river to be collected at low tide. Mudlarks were also banned from areas where ships were being coppered in case they stole the valuable copper. They could only look for nails and other items which had fallen into the river once the ships had gone.

Henry Mayhew met a group of twelve boy mudlarks gathered by one of the staircases leading down to the river, waiting for the tide to recede so they could start work. These children, whose ages ranged from six to twelve years, were huddled together in a muddy puddle.

It would be almost impossible to describe the wretched group, so motley was their appearance, so extraordinary their dress and so stolid and inexpressive their countenances ... There did not appear to be among the whole group as many filthy cotton rags to their backs as, when stitched together, would have been sufficient to form the material of one shirt.[15]

Mayhew interviewed one of the boys in this group, the nine-year-old son of a deceased coal-backer. The boy's mother worked as a charwoman and washerwoman when she could find work. His earnings of 1*d* to 4*d* a day were vital for their survival. He told Mayhew that:

> He had been three years mud-larking, and supposed he should remain a mud-lark all his life. What else could he be? for there was nothing else that he knew how to do.[16]

One reason for this boy's limited job options was his lack of education; he had only attended school for one month. Like so many street children, his knowledge was confined to what was necessary for his survival, as indicated by his response when questioned about God; 'God was God ... He had heard he was good, but didn't know what good he was to him.'[17] God was irrelevant to this boy's life. His knowledge of geography was also very limited; 'London was England, and England, he said, was in London, but he couldn't tell in what part.'[18]

Mayhew questioned all the street children he interviewed about their education. He was very concerned about the ignorance displayed by so many of them because he knew that without education they had little hope of ever escaping their dreadful lives. Many members of the middle class, however, would not have been as perturbed as Mayhew about this because of the anxiety, which had persisted since the French Revolution, that if the lower classes were educated too much they might rise up and rebel against their lot in life. Their lack of education helped to keep them in a subordinate position at the bottom of the social pyramid. There was a paradox here because, in order to become more civilised and acceptable members of society, the poor needed to be educated. However, if they became better educated the lower classes would have posed a different sort of threat to their social superiors than they did already. The poor could not win. They were damned if they remained ignorant and uncivilised and were also damned if they tried to follow the middle-class tenets of self-help and self-improvement by becoming educated.

Another boy interviewed by Mayhew was a 'quick, intelligent'[19] fourteen-year-old who had also been a mudlark for three years. He worked in a group of twenty to thirty boys. Mayhew spoke to both this boy and his mother. Despite the fact that it was 'the depth of winter' he was 'nearly destitute of clothing'[20] and his bare legs and feet were covered in chilblains. He was one of the three children of a coal-whipper who had suffered an accident at work while drunk which eventually led to his death. The family's plight had been bad enough during the father's lifetime but when he died they became desperate. They only survived because some kind neighbours scraped together enough money to enable the boy's mother to open a greengrocer's shop. The family managed well for five years and the children had even been able to attend school. Due to a run of bad luck, however, the greengrocery business failed and the boy had to find work. His mother was forced through ill-health to depend totally on what her son brought home from the river. In tears, she told Mayhew:

> And hard enough he had to work for what he got, poor boy ... still he never complained, but was quite proud when he brought home enough for us to get a bit of meat with; and when he has sometimes seen me downhearted, he has clung round my neck, and assured me that one day God would see us cared for if I would put my trust in Him.[21]

This young boy supported his family until his mother could work again. There was yet another setback, however, when he could not work for three months after a copper nail became embedded in his foot.

The little mudlark told Mayhew about the kindness shown to him by the masters of a ragged school he attended and how he had become involved with a gang of thieves he met there. Mayhew was worried about what this may lead to and decided to help him.

> I was so much struck with the boy's truthfulness of manner, that I asked him, would he really lead a different life, if he saw a means of so doing? He assured me he would, and begged me earnestly to try him.[22]

The result was that Mayhew found him a job in an office, where he thrived, and also found his sister work as a domestic servant. The boy did well enough to be able to set his mother up in a little shop and the family were back on their feet again.

This story provides another example of how some families had no choice but to rely on the efforts of their children to survive in London at this time. Like many others, this boy was forced to exchange places with his mother and support her financially and emotionally. His experiences also illustrate the precarious lives of the underclass and how their fate could turn on a period of good or bad luck. It provides further evidence of the uncomplaining stoicism with which the street children and their families faced repeated adversity, the temptations to which they were exposed and the resilience of the human spirit. It also shows how the poor often helped each other out in a crisis.

It was fortunate that this boy met Mayhew just at the point when he appeared to be turning from an honest, hard-working street child into the much-feared feral type. Mayhew concluded by saying that this was an example of how street children, when given the chance, could do well and earn an honest living.

> This simple story requires no comments, and is narrated here in the hope that it may teach many to know how often the poor boys reared in the gutter are thieves, merely because society forbids them being honest lads.[23]

CHAPTER 5

Street Entertainers and Street Labourers

I've been sweeping the crossings getting on for two years. Before that I used to go caten-wheeling after the buses. I don't like the sweeping, and I don't think there's e'er a one of us wot likes it. In the winter we has to be out in the cold, and then in summer we have to sleep out all night or go asleep on the church-steps, reg'lar tired out.

The King of the Tumbling-boy Crossing-sweepers' story

After twelve at night we goes to the Regent's Circus, and we tumbles there to the gentlemen and ladies. The most I ever got was sixpence at a time. The French ladies never give us nothink, but they all says "Chit, chit, chit," like hissing at us, for they can't understand us, and we're as bad off with them.

Young Mike's statement
Extracts taken from Henry Mayhew
London Labour and the London Poor, 1851

The streets of London in the early to mid-Victorian period offered an amazing array of entertainments and diversions. The colour, noise and excitement of these attractions created a lively carnival atmosphere. There was plenty for tourists, day-trippers, shoppers, workers on their lunch breaks, residents and passers-by to watch and enjoy. Street entertainers had been part of the London scene for centuries; their origins dated back to medieval fairs such as St Bartholomew's Fair in Smithfield.

There were street performers from many different countries, reflecting the cosmopolitan nature of the capital's population, including German bands, Irish bagpipers, Scottish dancers and Italian puppeteers. Performing, like costermongering, was often a hereditary occupation and many children were taught to perform from a young age. It was an arduous way to earn a living, like other street occupations. Entertainers worked long hours, in all weathers, and often walked many miles every day, carrying heavy equipment. The rewards were usually poor, especially in the winter months. People who stopped to watch performances often disappeared when the money collection was taken. Street entertainers, no doubt because they were so numerous, were regarded by some people as a nuisance and being harassed, jeered at, mocked and insulted were occupational hazards. Puppet shows, for example, were regularly spoiled by hordes of mischievous children who followed the performers from street to street and delighted in obstructing the show. It was also hard to stay cheerful and upbeat when hungry and worn down by the struggle to survive, as many performers were. One melancholy-looking and semi-starved street clown told Henry Mayhew that he had many times been forced to 'play the clown and indulge in all kinds of buffoonery, with a terrible heavy heart.'[1] He also pointed out how difficult it was to get out of the street business, which he described as 'a curse'. This man was one of many compelled to do work he detested because the only alternatives were the workhouse or starvation.

Street entertainers included musicians, dancers, puppeteers, jugglers, clowns, acrobats or 'tumblers', tightrope and stilt-walkers, strolling actors, reciters and performing animals. Like the street vendors, some performers worked in the same place every day and others travelled around, stopping to perform at different places, including residential streets. Certain locations became well-known for a particular form of entertainment. Leicester Square and Regent Street, for example, were famous for Punch and Judy shows, Oxford Street and Tottenham Court Road were favoured by the Fantoccini puppeteers and Gray's Inn Road by the fire-eaters. Street entertainment was also provided by exhibitors, or showmen, who demonstrated instruments such as telescopes, microscopes and thermoscopes for a penny-a-go. A popular microscope attraction was located near the London Hospital in Whitechapel. Other street attractions included peepshows, mechanical figures, waxworks, freakshows, roundabouts, swing-boats and street artists.

Musicians formed one of the largest groups of street entertainers. There were estimated to be more than 250 bands and a total of a thousand musicians on the streets of London at this time.[2] These included hurdy-gurdy players, organ-grinders, bell-ringers, cornet players and singers. Many Londoners regarded street musicians as disturbers of the peace and little better than beggars. Musicians were renowned for playing badly so they would be paid to go away. Max Schlesinger, in his book *Saunterings In and Around London*, described the 'unharmonious concert of two barrel organs' that could be heard amid the hubbub of the street. One was 'grinding out a woful caricature of the Marseillaise' while the other was making an 'awful screech.'[3] A Metropolitan Police Act of 1864 tried, with limited success, to deal with the nuisance caused by street musicians.

If trying to survive by performing on the streets was tough for adults, how much harder must it have been for children, especially the younger ones and those without a family? Once again, Mayhew's articles for *The Morning Chronicle* provide the best historical source on the lives of these children. Child entertainers often worked with their parents, as part of a family band or troupe, or with other adults. Some were sent out to perform by their parents, alone or with siblings. Others, without family or friends, worked alone.

Henry Mayhew met an eleven-year-old boy who worked as both a street performer and street labourer. His real name was Johnny, but he was known as the 'King of the Tumbling Boy Crossing Sweepers' or simply the 'King'. He belonged to a gang of boys who swept road crossings around St Martin's church in Trafalgar Square during the day and worked as street tumblers by night. The 'King' was:

> ... a pretty-looking boy ... with a pair of grey eyes that were as bright and clear as drops of sea-water. He was clad in a style in no way agreeing with his royal title; for he had on a kind of dirt-coloured shooting-coat of tweed, which was fraying into a kind of cobweb at the edges and elbows. His trousers too, were rather faulty, for there was a pink-wrinkled dot of flesh at one of the knees; while their length was too great for his majesty's short legs, so that they had to be rolled up at the end like a washer-woman's sleeves.[4]

This boy was an orphan who had been taken in by his grandmother and aunt and, therefore, had adults to care for him and a roof over his head, albeit only a single room in a slum tenement. He gave all his takings of up to a shilling a day to his grandmother. The 'King's' nickname and reputation were due to his superior ability at performing 'cat'en wheels' (Catherine wheels), being able to do them twelve or fourteen times running. This particular form of 'tumbling' was a better money spinner than less spectacular turns, such as head over heels, which the public had tired of. He willingly demonstrated his tumbling skills to Mayhew.

> He could bend his little legs round till they curved like the long German sausages we see in the ham-and-beef shops; and when he turned head over heels, he curled up his tiny body as closely as a wood-louse, and then rolled along, wabbling (sic) like an egg.[5]

The boy informed Mayhew that he 'worked hard for what he earned'. After sweeping crossings from mid-day, which he did not enjoy, especially in winter, the 'King' made his way to Covent Garden, The Haymarket and Pall Mall to perform 'tumbles' for drunken people leaving the theatres late in the evening. Only one in ten people gave him money, usually threepence or sixpence. Often, all the 'King' and his fellow acrobats received for their efforts was a kick or a blow; 'Some of the drunken gentlemens is shocking spiteful and runs after a chap and gives us a cut with his cane'.[6]

The tumblers also had to contend with hostile policemen who attacked them with their tunic belt-buckles 'but we generally gives 'em the lucky dodge and gets out of their way.'[7] They were regularly mocked and laughed at. Sometimes they went into shops and cafés to perform for customers, much to the fury of shopkeepers.

In the summer months the 'King' often slept out with the homeless members of his gang on the steps or in the doorway of St Martin's church. Most of his comrades had to choose between food and shelter in a lodging house, as they could not afford both. The gang, who had affectionate nicknames for each other, stuck together and had an agreed set of rules by which they worked. Occasional disagreements were settled by fights, with the rest of the gang watching to ensure fair play.

This chatty, lively and spirited boy was another street child who in many ways did not fit the stereotypical image, despite his cheekiness. He was polite, articulate, hard-working and did not appear to suffer unduly from the harshness of working and spending much of his life on the London streets. His cheerfulness was probably due to the camaraderie and support he enjoyed from being part of a gang. Mayhew admired this plucky and endearing boy.

Another story related by Mayhew shows how adults who had fallen on hard times were often forced to rely on their children in the battle to survive in early to mid-Victorian London. The Scottish dancing girl performed on the streets with her father, a blind bagpiper. The girl did not speak to Mayhew herself but an insight into her plight can be gleaned from her father's life story, which he told Mayhew in great detail. The bagpiper had once been a corporal in a highland regiment, holding a much sought-after and respected position as a colonel's orderly. He had led an active, interesting and adventurous life with no financial worries. However, this man had suffered a sudden and unexpected reversal of fortune when his eyesight began to fail and he had to retire from the army. Despite ten years of unblemished service, including fighting in two battles in India, he was not entitled to a pension. His anxiety to assure Mayhew that he had been a successful soldier and a man of good character reveals how acutely he felt his loss of status. A slight change in circumstances or a spell of bad luck often resulted in people sliding down the social scale in Victorian England.

Since leaving the army this man had earned his living as a wandering bagpipe player, accompanied by ten-year-old Maria, who danced as he played. 'My daughter dances the Highland Fling and the sword-dance' he told Mayhew. 'She does it pretty.'[8] They spent part of the year in London and the remainder performing around England and Scotland in order to support a large family. They travelled on foot because otherwise they would have missed the little off-road villages. The man's wife remained in London, doing her best to keep the family together with the help of a son who earned a shilling a day.

The bagpiper, who clearly loved his daughter, was acutely aware of how hard her life was, how exhausted she was from travelling and dancing, and how much she suffered from exposure to the elements. He was also worried about the risks involved in her performing a dangerous sword-dance, presumably included to make their act stand out from the countless other street performances. However, they had no alternative and their travels were usually worthwhile, especially when they visited garrison towns where people were willing to help an old soldier. The bagpiper assured Mayhew that he never asked for money but waited to be given it. This proud man did not want to be thought of as a beggar. He was anxious to be as respectable as possible and stated that he was a teetotaller who did not play in pubs because 'I don't like such places'.[9] He was a decent man striving to maintain his dignity as he struggled to support his family in impossible circumstances.

The Scottish dancing girl's life was harsh and gruelling. However, like the tumbling boy crossing-sweeper, she was more fortunate than many street children because she had a loving family, lodgings while travelling and some sort of home to return to. Her story shows that, although some street children were treated indifferently or even cruelly by adults, others were loved and looked after. Many of these caring adults no doubt, like the blind bagpiper, were not happy that the children in their care had to work on the streets.

Another way for the poor, both adults and children, to scrape a living was by providing one of a wide range of services offered on the streets of the capital at this time. These often self-employed people serviced the ever growing population of London and its visitors. Their cries, such as 'knives to grind' and 'umbrellas to mend', added to the cacophony of the streets. Some of the services required a varying degree of skill. These included the mending of articles such as china, clocks and chairs as well as the cleaning of hats, knives, scissors and other small items. Others, such as street porters and the linkmen who guided people through the London fog with torches, offered services requiring little or no skill. Some were employed, often during the night, by companies providing a public service and had the security of a regular wage. Dustmen, street disinfectors, street orderlies, night-soilmen, rubbish collectors and lamplighters fell into this category. Many poor citizens, therefore, contributed to the economy and prosperity of the Victorian capital as well as providing vital services to the community.

Children who worked as street labourers generally provided services which required no training or skill, a minimum of equipment and little or no start-up costs, such as running errands and holding horses. As with other street occupations, they had to compete with adults for business. Children frequently combined street labouring with other occupations to increase their earnings.

One service provided by street children was guiding people by torchlight through Victorian London's famous 'pea-souper' fogs. These were caused by fog mixing with smoke from innumerable coal fires and vapour from defective drains and the sewage-filled Thames. Sometimes, the fog hung around all day long. It varied in colour from white to yellow to bottle green depending on the temperature and was particularly bad in winter. At times, this fog was so pervasive that it insinuated itself into buildings. It helped to create the mysterious, threatening atmosphere of night-time Victorian London so vividly evoked by contemporary journalists, novelists and artists. Gas lamps and torches punctuated this thick blanket and added to the spookiness.

An American visitor to the capital in 1862 likened the fog to a 'solid wall constantly opposing our further progress.'[10] He could barely see the fingers of his outstretched hand. Apart from the obvious dangers of people losing their way or being knocked over and vehicles colliding, the fog made it easier for criminals to operate. Pickpockets and muggers could creep up on unsuspecting victims and disappear quickly into the enveloping fog once they had achieved their objective. The link-men and boys who sold torches and charged a few pennies to light the way for people therefore provided a very useful service. The American visitor of 1862 left the following description of the ragged link-boys:

> It was an amusing sight to see scores of ragged boys, carrying about torches for sale. The cry of "Links, links!" resounded on all sides. "Light you home for sixpence, sir", said one of them, as I stood watching their operations. "If 'tan't far", he added presently, "I'll light you for a joey" (4*d*).[11]

As with other street occupations, not all who worked as link-boys were honest. Anyone foolish enough to pay up front risked being cheated, as some rogues pocketed the money and slipped away into the fog without providing a service.

Sweeping crossings was a common occupation for street children. The only equipment required was a broom, although these had to be replaced regularly because they wore out quickly. Some child sweepers worked alone and others worked in gangs, like the St Martin's church gang. Some children went out, or were sent out by their parents, only on wet days when they were more likely to make money. In 1851 the number of children doing this work increased considerably when there was a huge influx of visitors to London for the Great Exhibition.

In his diary of 1862, Arthur Munby described a fourteen-year-old crossing sweeper named Margaret Cochrane. This girl, who looked older than her age, had for many years swept a path from King Charles' statue, near Charing Cross Road, to Spring Gardens. This was the busiest stretch of the road and was always thronged by 'hurrying carriages'.[12] Munby, an odd character with highly questionable motives for observing and speaking to female street workers, was in the habit of watching Margaret. Shabbily dressed in thin clothes which were often soaked through and splashed with mud, Margaret boldly swept under carriage wheels and dodged horses' hooves. Whatever his motives, Munby's diary is a useful and interesting source of information about the Victorian metropolis.

As with other street workers, the most detailed and revealing accounts of child street labourers are to be found in Mayhew's journalism. Among those he met was Ellen, another fourteen-year-old crossing sweeper, who worked in Trafalgar Square by a statue on horseback. Unusually for a street child, Ellen was a 'clean washed little thing' with 'a pretty expressive countenance, and each time she was asked a question she frowned, like a baby in its sleep, while thinking of the answer.'[13] Ellen's clothing was as ragged and inadequate as that of the other children Mayhew met:

> A cotton velvet bonnet, scarcely larger than the sun-shades worn at the sea-side, hung on her shoulders, leaving exposed her head, with the hair as rough as tow. Her green stuff gown was hanging in tatters, with long three-cornered rents as large as penny kites, showing the grey lining underneath; and her mantle was separated into so many pieces that it was only held together by the braiding at the edge.[14]

Ellen was born in Liquorpond Street, off Gray's Inn Lane, a slum area which was later cleared to make way for the railway. She was the daughter of a deceased Irish bricklayer whose widow died a year after him in a cholera epidemic. The orphaned child was given a home by her grandparents but had to find work as a cleaner and child minder to support herself. When her employers emigrated, Ellen was sent out by her grandmother to sell and to beg. She told Mayhew that:

> At last, finding I didn't get much at begging, I thought I'd go crossing sweeping. I saw other children doing it. I says to myself, "I'll go and buy a broom", and I spoke to another little girl, who was sweeping up Holborn, who told me what I was to do.[15]

At first Ellen was frightened of the fast cabs and carriages and her hands were sore from sweeping. Eventually she joined a gang of boy sweepers in Trafalgar Square. She stated that:

> It's a capital crossing, but there's so many of us, it spiles it. I seldom gets more than sevenpence a day, which I always takes home to grandmother.[16]

While constantly on the look-out for the police, this girl solicited gratuities with the words 'If you please, sir, give a poor girl a halfpenny'. She worked long hours with only Sundays off. Saturday was the best day of the week for her because that was when men, who were always more generous than women, were paid. Some Saturdays she earned 'perhaps ninepence but not quite a shilling'.[17]

Although forced by her circumstances to the hard life of a London street-child, this well-spoken and cheerful girl did not appear to be unhappy. She was another apparently well brought up child who contradicted the stereotypical image of the street child. Like so many others, she accepted her lot in life bravely and without a trace of self-pity. Having a home to return to, and a grandmother she was clearly attached to, must have helped to ease her plight.

To attract business, some sweepers resorted to decorating their crossings and this became quite a craze. Mayhew interviewed the lad who claimed to have started this custom. This confident and rather garrulous young man, who went by the nickname of 'the Goose', was the leader of the 'Tumbling Boy Crossing Sweepers'. He told Mayhew that he had been inspired by a man in Adelaide Street, off the Strand, who made money from ladies getting into and out of carriages by drawing pictures in the mud by the kerb-stone.

> I used to be at the crossing at the corner of Regent-suckus; and that's the wery place where I fust did it. The wery fust thing as I did was a hanker (anchor) – a regular one, with turn-up sides and a rope down the centre and all. I sweeped it away clean in the mud in the shape of the drawing I'd seen. It paid well, for I took one-and-ninepence on it. The next thing I tried was writing "God save the Queen"; and that, too, paid capital, for I think I got two bob. After that I tried We Har (V.R.) and a star, and that was a sweep too.[18]

However, when this enterprising boy went on to light up his crossing with farthing candles, the police stepped in and put a stop to it. He was threatened with being locked up for 'destructing the thoroughfare',[19] because of the disturbance caused when carriages slowed down and people stopped to look. This happy-go-lucky lad, another who fell into the hard-working, honest category of street child, appeared to enjoy life on the streets. He liked the challenge of keeping one step ahead of the hated police and admitted that he could have earned more if he had not larked around so much.

Another popular way for children to eke out a living on London's streets at this time was by cleaning shoes. If a child could find enough money to buy a shoe-cleaning kit, there were plenty of potential customers walking the dirty, dusty streets. The cry of 'a penny to clean your boots' was constantly heard in the capital. It is sad and ironic to note from contemporary photographs and cartoons that child shoe-blacks often did not possess any shoes of their own. These children, the majority of whom were boys, came from the same social backgrounds as children engaged in other street occupations. Many came from the slum homes in St Giles' parish, including the most run down and overcrowded districts such as Five Dials and Seven Dials.

After 1851 most of the city's boy shoe-blacks belonged to the London Shoe-Black Society, also known as the Ragged Shoe-Black Society. The establishment of this organisation was one of the early attempts to do something to help the street children. The boys, who formed eight uniformed brigades of 350 members each, were mostly aged twelve to thirteen. They worked as shoe-blacks by day and attended ragged schools in the evenings and on Sunday mornings.

Unfortunately, the existence of the London Shoe-Black Society made life difficult for independent child shoeblacks. Adolphe Smith in *Street Life in London* claimed that, although the shoe-black brigades were an 'excellent institution', they had 'decidedly trespassed on the freedom of the street industries.'[20] The brigades, with the support of the police, eventually monopolised the best beats and pitches. Brigade boys came to be regarded as the legitimate shoe-blacks and the police could not see why all boys did not want to join them. However, many boys did not want to be subjected to the discipline of belonging to a brigade, as the great attraction of street life for them was the freedom and independence it allowed them.

Independent shoe-blacks were compelled to buy a licence costing five shillings a year and anyone who failed to comply was badly treated by the police. Procuring a licence was not easy, however, with preference being given to the old and disabled. Independent shoe-blacks, like itinerant street-sellers, were constantly watched and harassed by police. They were made to keep on the move and were only allowed to put down their shoe-shine box when they had found a customer. The police did not always succeed, as a few independent shoe-blacks were supported by traders and shopkeepers who knew them. However, those who were left alone were the exception. As Smith concluded, 'only boys of the brigade and old men and cripples are welcome to practise the art of cleaning boots in the streets of the metropolis.'[21] The odds were therefore stacked against many street children who tried to make a living this way.

Many children were so ground down by life on the streets that they did not have the time, energy or desire to take advantage of London's leisure opportunities and street entertainment. Some, however, did seek occasional respite from their tough lives. A popular amusement among the better-off children, who could afford the cost of entrance and refreshments, was the 'penny gaff'. These makeshift theatres were set up in former shops and the back rooms of public houses in the poor districts. Up to six performances a night were held in some establishments. Alcohol was usually freely available.

In *Here and There in London,* published in 1859, J. Ewing Ritchie described these places as 'dirty holes'.[22] He visited one of the worst, in the New Cut off Waterloo Road, and was horrified to discover what 'indecent, disgusting and violent'[23] entertainment was on offer. To see how much the 'half-grown girls and boys'[24] understood and enjoyed the lewd show disturbed him greatly.

Henry Mayhew, who was as concerned about the moral and spiritual welfare of the street children as the physical, also visited a penny gaff. He was aware of the moral depravity of many of these children, which was partly due to being left to their own devices. They lacked the good example and moral guidance usually provided by parents and the Church. Mayhew was anxious to investigate other moral influences on these unprotected children and, in order to do so, attended one of the least offensive shows, at a penny gaff near Smithfield. He mingled with the excited crowd of girls in 'showy cotton velvet polkas' with 'dowdy feathers in their crushed bonnets'[25] and pipe smoking, whistling, laughing boys. The police were present to preserve order. As the doors opened to let out the audience from the previous performance, Mayhew was hit by an indescribable stench and then was pushed and shoved by the yelling crowd, eager to get in. The filthy language as well as the immoral and violent content of the show horrified Mayhew, who described it as 'a platform to teach the cruellest debauchery ... things are acted and spoken that it is criminal even to allude to.'[26]

The young members of this audience included some of the 'better class' of street child as well as the more feral element. Mayhew did not condemn them for seeking relief from their grinding work, troubles and fatigue in such unseemly places. Instead, he blamed society in general for not providing the poor and vulnerable with wholesome entertainment and the 'venal traders'[27] whose shows appealed only to the brutal instincts of those watching. He was deeply concerned for the children caught up in such depravity. The escape provided by the penny gaffs was, however, only temporary. The children seen by Ritchie and Mayhew were soon back with the other street children, battling against hunger, fatigue, temptation, the elements and the indifference of the more fortunate in the endless battle to stay alive.

Henry Mayhew was largely responsible for alerting society to the plight of London's street children in all its sordid detail. His readers must have shared his shock at the discoveries he made about the child street sellers, scavengers, performers and labourers. The better-off classes were aware of the need for poor children to work but the dangers and bad influences they were exposed to, their independence and their premature assumption of adult responsibilities would have been a startling revelation. They would also have been shocked at the harsh reality of the lives and suffering of these children, all the more powerful for being expressed in their own words. The inclusion of the names, physical descriptions and the occasional illustration of individual children further authenticated these revelations. To the children themselves, of course, this suffering was normal because most of them had known no other life. This was why they were so matter of fact about the hardships they endured.

Mayhew's articles were also important because they showed the positive characteristics displayed by a number of street children and how unfair the accepted image of them was. It must have been reassuring to his readers that not all these children fitted the feral stereotype and many were in some respects closer to the middle-class ideal of childhood than they could possibly have imagined.

CHAPTER 6

Criminal Children

There are thousands of neglected children loitering about the low neighbourhoods of the metropolis, and prowling about the streets, begging and stealing for their daily bread. They are to be found in Westminster, Whitechapel, Shoreditch, St.Giles's, New Cut, Lambeth, the Borough, and other localities. Hundreds of them may be seen leaving their parents' homes and low lodging houses every morning sallying forth in search of food and plunder.

Henry Mayhew
London Labour and the London Poor, 1851

It would often be better if children had no parents at all.

Lord Shaftesbury

Fears about the ever increasing level of crime in London centred around a visible and menacing underclass, of which juveniles formed a large proportion. The social investigative journalists drew attention to the threat these criminal juveniles posed and their behaviour became the subject of widespread concern and condemnation. Many people believed that crime was hereditary and it was feared that this class was perpetually reproducing itself. The presence of these criminals was also a stain on the reputation of the great metropolis.

In a letter to *The Morning Chronicle* dated 19 March 1850, Henry Mayhew produced statistical tables that showed the alarming increase in juvenile crime in London. The statistics he used expressed juvenile crime in terms of those taken into custody. Mayhew summarised his findings by stating that:

In 1839 ... only 1 youth in 53 was taken into custody; in 1848 the ratio had risen to 1 in 47. In 1845 the proportion was 1 in 51, and since that date it has gradually increased to 1 in 47.[1]

Concern about London's homeless and destitute juveniles became so great that in 1852 a government select committee was appointed to look into the problem. This led to a government contribution to an emigration scheme for juveniles put forward by Lord Shaftesbury, but otherwise made very little difference to the problem. In 1869 James Greenwood recorded that:

> Within the limits of our vast and wealthy city of London, there wander, destitute of proper guardianship, food, clothing, or employment, a hundred thousand boys and girls in fair training for the treadmill and the oakum shed, and finally for Portland and the convict's mark.[2]

In the same year, Thomas Archer described the wretched physical appearance of these ubiquitous children who existed 'continually on the borders of crime'.

> ... you may listen to their foul words and see their crouching, shuddering bodies, their wasted limbs and old-young faces; worn with the want of food, and the wild wistful wonder of how they are to keep on living, or whether it would be better to die.[3]

The streets of London were dangerous and there were many no-go areas, such as the Seven Dials slum district, which even the police were afraid to enter. Common crimes included beggary, debauchery, theft, burglary, mugging, highway robbery, assault and murder. Many crimes were fuelled by drunkenness, one of James Greenwood's *Seven Curses of London*. Victims of crime ranged from young children, who were vulnerable to robbery by other children as they ran errands, as well as kidnapping and abduction, to the wealthy victims of pickpockets and thieving prostitutes. The link between poverty, its associated environmental factors and crime were recognised at this time and confirmed by the findings of the early social investigative journalists.

Many of the street children were criminals. Some were habitual criminals who belonged to the feral category of street child but others turned to crime because of the difficulties of earning a living honestly in London. Many of the poorest children were thin, weak, under-sized, emaciated, depressed and in bad health. They were physically unable to do labouring jobs and much of the other casual work in the metropolis. A lack of skills and basic education were further disadvantages. For many, therefore, the only options were the workhouse or crime. Due to the shame, disgrace and fear associated with the former, the latter was often the only option left. Some children resorted to crime only when desperate and returned to honest work as soon as they could. Some normally honest children only succumbed to the temptation of crime when the opportunity presented itself. There were plenty of temptations and easy pickings on the streets.

Juvenile criminals came from similar backgrounds to the street children who struggled to survive by honest means but, not surprisingly, those born into criminal families were most likely to become criminals themselves. These children knew no other way of acquiring the necessities of life than by stealing. James Greenwood described such children as having been 'bred and nurtured'[4] in crime. They had inherited criminal dispositions from their parents in the same way as certain forms of physical disease could be inherited. Greenwood considered that such children could not be blamed for their criminality as it had not been of their own choosing. There were so many children in this category that they swarmed 'like mites in rotten cheese'[5] throughout London. Greenwood pointed out that, oddly, these children were not actually trained to steal by fathers who were hardened criminals. What happened to them, he concluded, was much worse – they were never taught the difference between right and wrong.

> ... if in the benighted den in which he is born, and in which his childish intellect dawns, no ray of light and truth ever penetrates, and he grows into the use of his limbs and as much brains as his brutish breeding affords him, and with no other occupation before him than to follow in the footsteps of his father the thief – how much more hopeless is his case.[6]

Neglected children were also liable to turn to crime. Either their parents did not know, or did not care, what they were doing, or they were working long hours and were unable to supervise their offspring.

Children who had been thrown out of, or had run away, from their homes were also likely to become criminals. One boy described himself to Henry Mayhew as 'totally destitute' after being thrown out of doors, 'a little boy in the great world of London'.[7] For many such children a life of crime was better than the abuse, neglect and indifference they had endured at home. Children subjected to abuse or exploitation at this period had no legal rights or redress and usually no-one to turn to. Most adults, and society in general, were not concerned about the suffering of poor children.

Some children sent out by their parents to supplement the family income, or even support the entire family while their parents shirked, often resorted to crime. Some parents actively encouraged, or even forced, their children to commit crime because once convicted, a child became the responsibility of the parish.[8] Many parents were not bothered how their children acquired money as long as they did so. Like some child street sellers, these children often risked a beating if they returned home without enough money and one way to acquire it quickly was by crime. In 1850 Henry Mayhew summed up the prospects of children from the very worst backgrounds.

> The children that survive noxious influences and awful neglect are thrown, as soon as they can crawl, to scramble in the gutter, and leave their parents to amusement or business; as they advance in years they discover that they must, in general, find

their own food or go without it. At an age when the children of the wealthy would still be in leading strings, they are off, singly or in parties, to beg, borrow, steal and exercise all the cunning that want and a love of evil can stir up in a reckless race.[9]

Another group of children likely to become criminals were those who had been orphaned or abandoned. These included the offspring of criminals in prison or transported, and very young children, many of them illegitimate, who had been dumped on the streets. Such children were often taken in by adult criminals and fed, clothed and sheltered in low lodging houses until they were old enough to steal themselves. Those not under the control of an adult were forced into crime to survive. These children lived wretched and tragic lives. James Greenwood described them as:

Sharpened by hunger, intimidated by severe treatment and rendered adroit by vigilant training, this class of thieves is perhaps the most numerous, the most daring, the cleverest and the most difficult to reform.[10]

The majority of children in the above categories had had no childhood at all. Charles Dickens pointed out that they had never received any parental love, smiles or endearments.

They have entered at once upon the stern realities and miseries of life ... Talk to *them* of parental solicitude, the happy days of childhood, and the merry games of infancy! Tell them of hunger and the streets, beggary and stripes, the gin-shop, the station-house, and the pawnbroker's and they will understand you.[11]

These children were the very antithesis of the protected, loved, cosseted and well behaved middle-class child. They had no moral bearings at all, having received no parental guidance or education from Church or school, and had no idea how to live an honest, respectable life. Never having had any possessions of their own, these children had no concept of property or ownership.[12] They could not see why it was wrong to take what belonged to others or why they were punished for doing what they needed to do in order to survive. Any who could grasp the idea of ownership reasoned that if others could have things, why shouldn't they?

Even children from better backgrounds, who had received some moral guidance, could be led astray by juvenile criminals they met on the streets. They saw that money could be obtained more quickly and easily by crime than the long, hard slog of selling, performing or doing casual work. Some decided that the risks involved in crime were worth taking to get the rewards.

Another cause of juvenile crime was the physical environment in which so many children grew up. The appalling conditions in the slums of London were the perfect breeding ground for child criminals. Many of these districts were so steeped in crime that they were beyond the control of the police. Any childhood innocence was soon lost in the slums. For many of these children the first words they learned were swear words.

One of the saddest passages written by Henry Mayhew records a walk through the notorious criminal districts of Southwark. Among the menacing criminals skulking on the streets and prostitutes hanging around on the look-out for business, he came across a group of laughing girls. These children were happily playing an innocent childhood game, apparently oblivious to their hideous surroundings and the vicious low-life around them.

> In the neighbourhood of the Mint we found a number of children gambolling in the streets. One in particular arrested our attention, an interesting little girl of about five years of age, with a sallow complexion, but most engaging countenance, radiant with innocence and hope. Other sweet little girls were playing by her side, possibly the children of some of the abandoned men and women of the locality. How sad to think of these young innocents exposed to the contamination of bad companionships around them, and to the pernicious influence of the bad example of their parents.[13]

Even children of honest parents struggling to survive in the slums were subjected to vile influences. Slum homes and lodging houses, as well as being physically filthy, dilapidated, verminous and overcrowded, were places of moral filth and degradation. All manner of disgusting behaviour was the norm in dwellings where privacy and decency were impossible. On the streets children witnessed brutality, drunkenness, wife beating, debauchery and violence as a matter of course.

The very worst vice and iniquity were to be found in the low lodging houses and a great deal of the crime committed in London was plotted in them. Any child lucky enough to have received lessons in honesty and morality soon forgot them on entering such places. Desperate, hungry, unwanted and bewildered street children were particularly vulnerable. Before long they started to drink, gamble, take part in deviant behaviour and resort to crime. They were often snapped up by resident beggar and thief masters because a small child not known to the police was a valuable asset. Young migrants from the countryside, with no experience of London and its dangers, were likely to be ensnared. Some of the worst lodging houses were in Bethnal Green, Whitechapel, the Borough and Gray's Inn Lane. The last named was the most notorious of the haunts of criminals, prostitutes and members of the London underworld. It was here that a lodging house described by Dickens as the 'Thieves Kitchen and Seminary for the Teaching of the Art to Children' was located.

Charles Dickens, Henry Mayhew and Thomas Archer all visited thieves' dens accompanied by police officers. Dickens paid a visit to a lodging house owned by a 'ferocious' villain and receiver of stolen goods named Bark who cursed and swore at being disturbed in the dead of night. His house was located in the 'innermost recesses of the worst part of London' and was 'crammed with notorious robbers and ruffians'.[14] Dickens was frightened even with the protection of the police. He described the meeting of criminals he witnessed in progress by lamplight there as 'by far the most dangerous assembly we have seen yet'.[15] Dickens was impressed by the professionalism of the police and noticed the grudging respect in which they were held by these hardened criminals. He also noticed, during this visit, the humanity of the Police Inspector who accompanied him in his dealings with the poor. Child criminals frequented flash houses and thieves' kitchens to meet each other socially, to plan crimes and dispose of stolen goods.

There was a strong connection between vagrancy and juvenile crime. The vagrant class was one of the main sources from which juvenile criminals were 'continually recruited and augmented'[16] according to Mayhew. Some stayed in the capital throughout the year, seeking shelter in lodging houses when they could afford to. Others belonged to an army of young vagrants who left London for the countryside each year as summer approached. They survived by means of casual work such as hopping and harvesting as well as begging and crime. Until 1848, when a stricter admissions system was introduced, these habitual vagrants progressed around the country from casual ward to casual ward. Their violent and destructive behaviour frightened away the people for whom the wards were intended.

In the winter these young vagrants returned to London and headed for the asylums for the houseless poor. Mayhew described vagrants as 'one of the most restless, discontented, vicious, and dangerous elements of society'.[17] Prison held no terror for this group of juveniles and many committed crimes to go there. Mayhew's investigations led him to conclude that the vast majority of vagrants had chosen this way of life because the effort and discipline which a job required was 'irksome' to them. They lacked the sense of purpose and discipline necessary to keep a job. Although some of these youngsters had been educated, the work ethic had never been instilled into them.

Another factor contributing to juvenile crime, according to Mayhew and his fellow journalists, was the influence on children of 'gutter' or 'gallows' literature which glorified violence and crime. 'Penny dreadful' magazines, which were sold in vast numbers in London every day, contained stories with titles such as 'Tyburn Dick' and 'The Boy Burglar'. A number of boys interviewed by Mayhew revered Jack Sheppard, a notorious eighteenth-century criminal and a hero of such literature. These stories were read by children who could read to those who could not. Thomas Archer, who was particularly vehement in his condemnation of what he called 'Devil's Primers', was pleased to find his views corroborated by the chaplain of a House of Detention in his annual report for 1870 to the magistrates for Middlesex.[18]

Begging was a common crime among children. Beggars were everywhere in the metropolis at this time and the police were probably harder on them than any other group of criminals. Despite this, their numbers did not diminish as the century progressed. Many adult beggars were professionals who chose to beg rather than try to find work. They adopted all sorts of tricks to gain sympathy and money from the public. These able-bodied people were the equivalent of the 'sturdy beggar' of Elizabethan times. Their 'dodges' included pretending to be blind or disabled, or posing as out of work labourers or craftsmen or down at heel gentlemen. Some even borrowed children to pose as destitute family men. Many did well out of begging. These fakes made it very difficult for those who genuinely had no choice between begging and the workhouse. The Mendicity Society, founded in 1818, whose headquarters were in Red Lion Square, off Holborn, did its best to stamp out professional begging and to help those in genuine need.

Child beggars were prolific on the London streets. Some started begging with their parents at an early age as one of a family group; others were sent out alone by their parents. Street selling was often used as a front by child beggars. Among the genuine child sellers and boot blacks there were always children carrying a few boxes of matches, pins or flowers, or boot cleaning boxes as a cover. They would have been affronted if anyone tried to buy from them or asked for their boots to be cleaned, instead of just giving them money. Some carried brooms and posed as crossing sweepers so as not to be arrested. Very few directly solicited for money. Some children were sent out to 'whine for alms' by adult cadgers who watched at a distance and regularly relieved them of their takings. Henry Mayhew met many young beggars and noticed that, as a class, they were not very bright and were generally illiterate. If they had been more intelligent, he concluded, they would 'almost certainly' have been thieves.

The most common juvenile crimes were theft and pick-pocketing. The majority of thieves were boys who started thieving between the ages of five and seven, often by stealing food from street stalls. Hordes of ragged child thieves emerged from their slum homes and lodging houses early each morning and at dusk to search for food and to commit crime. They were seen loitering on streets throughout the metropolis or crouching on pavements, awaiting an opportunity to pick a pocket or steal. They stole from rich and poor alike. Mayhew noticed how intelligent and precocious these children usually were; they were much brighter, sharper and more cunning than child beggars. These juveniles spoke to each other in 'Thieves' Latin', imitating adult criminals. In this language a boy thief was known as a 'little snakesman', a thief trainer was a 'kidsman', to commit burglary was to 'crack a case' or 'break a drum' and a three-month prison sentence was a 'tailpiece'.

Pick-pocketing was a highly organised crime. Some pick-pockets worked independently, having learned the necessary skills from other street children, and others were schooled by thief trainers like Isaac (Ikey) Solomons, on whom the character of Fagin in *Oliver Twist* was modelled. These children handed over all their criminal gains to the adult controlling them. Pick-pockets varied in age and skillfulness. At one extreme was the ragged urchin who stole handkerchiefs out of back pockets; at the other extreme was the older lad dressed as a gentleman's son who stole gentlemen's watches and wallets from front pockets in the fashionable West End. Pick-pockets were always active where crowds gathered and people's attention was diverted, including public occasions and events, amusement venues, fires and accident scenes. They were much in evidence at the Great Exhibition, for example. Stolen goods could be disposed of for cash with no difficulty and no questions asked. Receivers included lodging house keepers, dolly shops (unlicensed pawnbrokers) as well as coffee shops, hairdressers and other small businesses in poor streets.

The story of one pick-pocket interviewed by Henry Mayhew illustrates how easy it was for a child to be drawn into crime and how inexorable was his progress towards becoming a hardened adult criminal. Mayhew described this young man as:

> ... of tolerably good education, and has a most intelligent mind, well furnished with reading and general information. At the time we met him he was rather melancholy and crushed in spirit, which he stated was the result of repeated imprisonments, and the anxiety and suspense connected with his wild criminal life, and the heavy trials he has undergone.[19]

He was the son of a Wesleyan minister with a good and loving home background but he had rebelled against his restricted religious upbringing. This boy left home for London at the age of ten, where he stayed at a lodging house until his money ran out. He then found himself destitute and alone on the streets.

Too proud to write to his parents for help, he was adopted by a gang of rough boys who survived by stealing handkerchiefs from the back pockets of male passengers alighting from boats at the Adelphi Stairs. This form of pick-pocketing was known as 'working at the tail' because the back pocket was under the coat tail. The boys slept, appropriately enough, in an old prison van without wheels parked under the arches of the Adelphi, a riverside development of terraced houses off the Strand. The new boy soon felt compelled to pick-pocket himself because he was ashamed to share his friends' food without helping. He became the best pickpocket in the gang and before long he received his first term of imprisonment.

Having progressed to the more lucrative picking of ladies' pockets, this lad was well on his way to a life of crime by the age of thirteen. Around this time he emulated his fellow thieves by cohabiting with a young girl and, as was the usual practice with young thieves, mistreated and beat her until she left him. She was the first of many cohabitees, prostitutes and criminals themselves, who added to the instability of his life. Over the next few years this young pick-pocket was in and out of prison constantly, but even a period of the silent punishment system failed to break him. Each time he was released he was met by his current gang members and began stealing again.

This lad's criminality was only curbed when he was aware of the police watching him. Attempts to seek honest work were hampered by his lack of skills or a trade and his criminal record. After moving on to burglary, he was eventually shocked into giving up crime when he narrowly escaped transportation. When he met Mayhew this boy was working as a patterer, someone who sold goods on the streets by using verbal patter. Having given up crime, his standard of living was much reduced and he was only just able to survive, or 'make a shift'[20] as he put it. He did not hold out much hope for the future but he had, at least, broken free from crime.

Shops and market stalls were common targets for child criminals, often working in pairs or small groups. One child would distract the stall-holder or shopkeeper while the others stole goods or raided the tills. Associates on the streets would trip up anyone who pursued the thief. Many shops displayed articles on tables outside, providing an open invitation to young thieves. Shoemakers were particularly vulnerable in this respect and often employed people to keep watch over their displays. Clothes were frequently stolen from shop dummies by children. In quiet back streets young thieves broke the windows of shops such as tobacconists and watchmakers to grab goods. In residential areas they even stole clothes and linen from washing lines. Opportunist child thieves stole from hotel lobbies, railway station concourses and parked vehicles.

Children also worked as 'sneak thieves'. They sneaked around basement courtyards, known as areas, in residential streets, especially in the West End. When an opportunity arose they dived into areas and raided provision safes or entered kitchens and stole whatever they could easily carry away. Boys often worked with adult burglars, as they were useful for climbing through windows and fanlights into shops, houses and warehouses. Many juveniles were proficient housebreakers and burglars by their early teens.

The river police were kept busy trying to catch thieving juvenile mudlarks. Many mudlarks did not confine themselves to legitimate items washed up on the shore but were thieves as well. One of these boys, the son of an Irish dock worker, told his story to Henry Mayhew. This 'strong and healthy'[21] thirteen-year-old, dressed in a brown fustian coat, greasy patched trousers, a striped shirt and cap, had been to school for three years. He told Mayhew:

> We are often chased by the Thames police and the watermen, as the mudlarks are generally known to be thieves. I take what I can get as well as the rest when I get an opportunity.[22]

This boy often boarded coal barges and knocked or threw coal into the mud to collect later, and stole articles from cabins. He was used to being chased by police galleys as illustrated by the following story:

> One day, about three o'clock in the afternoon, as I was at Young's Dock, I saw a large piece of copper drop down the side of a vessel which was being repaired. On the same evening, as a ship was coming out of the docks, I stripped off my

clothes and dived down several feet, seized the sheet of copper and carried it away, swimming by the side of the vessel. As it was dark, I was not observed by the crew nor by any of the men who opened the gates of the dock. I fetched it to the shore, and sold it that night to a marine store dealer.[23]

So far he had avoided being tried in court for any felony.

As particularly illustrated by the pick-pocket's story, it was very difficult for a child to break the cycle of crime. Certain factors encouraged children to continue offending. Thomas Archer made the perceptive observation that for most of these children the first proper attention they received from an adult was when they committed a crime. He pointed out that once recognised by the police and criminal justice system, children were treated with consideration which, if it had been given earlier 'while innocent and merely destitute, might have done them and the state some service'.[24] For many of these children the criminal gangs they belonged to were the only family they had and to give up crime would have led to the loss of such support and companionship.

The majority of juvenile criminals were boys but there were some girl criminals too. Although they tended to commit less serious crimes, girls were likely to become much more hardened criminals than boys. Society viewed female criminals more harshly than males because of the belief in the moral superiority of the female sex. It was considered, therefore, much more shameful for a girl to turn to crime. Girls either worked as accomplices to boy criminals, by acting as their look-outs or disposing of their ill-gotten gains, or they committed crime, usually theft, on their own. Some girls combined theft with prostitution, often by stealing from their clients.

Henry Mayhew met a number of young female criminals when he visited the girls' section of the Westminster House of Correction. The following extract is from a description of his visit in *The Criminal Prisons of London, and Scenes of Prison Life*, published in 1862.

The girl prisoners were clad in blue and white-spotted cotton frocks, and caps with deep frilled borders, and most of them had long strips of shiny straw plait dangling from their hands, which they kept working at instinctively with their little fingers, while they looked with wonder up into our face. Some, as usual, were pretty-looking creatures, that enlisted all one's sympathies, almost to tears, in their favour, whilst others had so prematurely brazen a look, that the heart shrunk back as we inwardly shuddered at the thought that our own little girl – half angel though she seem now – born in the same circumstances, and reared among the same associates, would assuredly have been the same young fiend as they.[25]

These children, the youngest of whom was only eight, were in prison for theft, pick-pocketing and, in the case of one girl, for passing bad money which her 'aunt' had given her to spend. Having heard the stories of these young girls, Mayhew questioned the wisdom of branding mere infants as thieves. He blamed their parents for allowing them to 'run wild in the streets' and society for failing to understand who was really at fault.

For the first half of the nineteenth century, prison was the government's only solution to juvenile crime. Conditions and punishments were harsh in order to act as a deterrent. Children were treated virtually the same as adults under the criminal justice system. Up to the age of seven children could not be held responsible for any criminal action, between the ages of seven and fourteen the prosecution had to prove a child's ability to tell the difference between good and evil, and children above the age of fourteen were deemed fully responsible for their actions. Boys as young as seven were often sentenced to imprisonment and by the age of twelve many had received six or more sentences. Children were imprisoned for minor offences such as theft of food or coal. Pick-pockets, usually repeat offenders, were sentenced to transportation.

The early social investigative journalists met many street children who had been subjected to the harsh Victorian penal code. The prison system, which included both correctional and detentional facilities, was three-tiered. Bridewells were used for sentences of up to three months, Houses of Correction for sentences of between three months and two years, and prisons for longer sentences. Tothill Fields Prison was specifically for women and children but juveniles were placed in male prisons too. There were also prison hulks in the Thames estuary, including the *Euryalis* for children. These obsolete warships housed those awaiting transportation and also served as overflow prisons. Many prisoners served their entire sentences in these verminous, overcrowded, rotting hulks as transportation ships were few and far between and there were many waiting for a place on them.

Prisons were grim and dreadful places for children. Juveniles were subjected to harsh deterrent regimes, including the silent system. Occasionally, children died as a result of punishment in prison. Punishments included solitary confinement, the straitjacket, the dark refractory cell, flogging, a restricted diet, oakum picking and time on an iron drum turned by a handle called a crank. Until 1847 boys and girls under fourteen could also be sentenced to time on the treadmill, a revolving wheel with steps which ground corn or empty air. Transportation for juveniles came to an end by 1853. Very few child criminals were executed during this period.

In 1847, with the passing of the Juvenile Offenders Act, children began to be treated differently to adults. Special courts were set up to deal with those under the age of fourteen and not long afterwards this was extended to under sixteens. This Act enabled some cases to be dealt with summarily by magistrates, for minor charges to be dismissed, and made it possible for juveniles to be treated more leniently than adults. However, this Act only applied to lesser offences.

The punitive prison system failed to stem the flood of juvenile crime and even acted as an incentive to commit crime. Despite the harsh regime of the prison system, it offered the benefits of food, warmth, shelter and clothing, which children struggled to provide for themselves. A spell in prison gave them a welcome respite from grim street life, and having once experienced its comparative comforts, including the chance to have a bath and a good night's sleep, children were often keen to return there. Those who received a long sentence for a bad crime were given a better diet than those serving shorter sentences. It was, therefore, worthwhile aiming for a longer sentence.

Another reason prison failed to deal with juvenile crime was that prisons became schools of crime. Juveniles learned from older, professional criminals with whom they associated while awaiting trial in remand prisons. Furthermore, harsh punishments such as flogging often only hardened young offenders and made them more determined to go on committing crime. Prisons did little more than keep these children in custody and off the streets for a while.

To many boys, a criminal record was a badge of honour. In January 1850 Mayhew called a meeting of 150 young criminals, typical of the feral type of street child, at a school room in Shadwell. Their pride in their repeated spells in prison was obvious. He left the following staggering record of offences committed by the juveniles who attended.

> 12 of the youths assembled had been in prison once (2 of these were but 10 years of age); 5 had been in prison twice; 3, thrice; 4, four times; 7, five times; 8, six times; 5, seven times; 4, eight times; 2, nine times (1 of them 13 years of age); 5, ten times; 5, twelve times; 2, thirteen times; 3, fourteen times; 2, sixteen times; 3, seventeen times; 2, eighteen times; 5, twenty times; 6, twenty-four times; 1, twenty-five times; 1, twenty-six times; and 1, twenty-nine times.[26]

As these prison records were called out, they were greeted 'with great applause, which became more and more boisterous as the number of imprisonments increased'.[27] The record of the nineteen-year-old who had been in prison twenty-nine times was received with prolonged clapping of hands, cat calls and shouts of 'bravo'. Some of those present were so proud of their criminal records that they had chalked on their hats the total number of their spells in prison.

Charles Dickens also saw for himself how the prison system failed juveniles. On a visit to Newgate Prison, a group was lined up for him to inspect.

> The whole number, without an exception, we believe, had been committed for trial on charges of pocket-picking; and fourteen such terrible little faces we never beheld. There was not one redeeming feature among them – not a glance of honesty – not a wink expressive of anything but the gallows and the hulks, in the whole collection. As to anything like shame or contrition, that was entirely out of the question.[28]

The journalists who investigated and wrote about juvenile crime in London at this time agreed that prison did not work. They, like many other members of the middle class, were also concerned about the moral influence and the effects of incarceration on the minds of children. Some journalists offered their own solutions to the problem. Dickens suggested that feckless parents should lose custody of their children and be forced to support them financially if they could afford to. Mayhew pointed out that attempts to make good citizens by the prevention or punishment of vice had failed. He argued that trying to deter crime through fear led only to negative results.

> It may prevent the criminal appetite or desire from being put into action, but it cannot possibly implant one virtuous desire in its stead.[29]

Mayhew's solution was a 'corrective method' of dealing with young criminals by cultivating virtue in them through education.

The long-term prospects for the child beggars and criminals who spent their lives on the London streets in the early to mid-Victorian period were grim. The former were most likely to become adult beggars or progress to crime, due to the scarcity of work and their lack of the work ethic. The latter were likely to become hardened adult criminals, often committing more vicious and violent crimes with regular imprisonment, transportation or even execution as punishment. Of these, transportation offered the best hope with a life away from former associates and the chance to start a new life on the other side of the world, once it had been earned. Children who continued on the path of crime were likely to see the cycle of deprivation, neglect and crime repeated in the next generation. A few child criminals were able to break away from crime and embark on an honest life.

The stark revelations of the early social investigative journalists stirred up the growing unease about London's 'dangerous classes'. Fears were deepened by graphic descriptions of slums, low lodging houses, savage children, the criminal underworld and the failing prison system. Mayhew's detailed accounts of the different crimes children were involved in and how they carried out their crimes must have been particularly alarming. Furthermore, his accounts were authenticated by stories of child criminals in their own words.

The language used by journalists added to readers' fears. They wrote, for example, of 'swarms' or 'armies' of feral juvenile criminals emerging from their 'lairs' or 'haunts'. Many members of the higher classes already had first-hand experience of crimes committed by children as victims of pickpockets, thieves, muggers and burglars. These factors combined to create a deep anxiety about the future of the city. There was also, in the background, the lurking worry that the lowest classes might rise up and rebel, which had been recently re-awakened by Chartist agitation in London for universal manhood suffrage, and revolutions in some European cities. The feral type of street children, described so vividly by social investigative journalists, were not only a threat to a law-abiding society and civil order but were also an outrage to moral decency. As well as being unpleasant, even repulsive to look at, with their matted hair, dirty faces and ragged clothes, they were also rude, foul-mouthed, disrespectful, badly behaved and defiant of adult control.

Fear and alarm continued to grow about the rapidly increasing juvenile crime rate. Reaching its peak in the late 1850s, it became clear that the government had no choice but to take action. A number of social surveys around the middle of the century confirmed the link between childhood deprivation and crime which had already been drawn to the public's attention by journalists and other writers. It began to be accepted that criminal children needed to be rescued and helped by means of education and training rather than locked up. Social reformers, such as Mary Carpenter, who worked with street children in Bristol, also called for a more humane approach towards young offenders and for more account to be taken of the fact that they were not responsible for their own actions. The result was a move towards reforming young criminals rather than just punishing them.

The government responded by passing the Young Offenders Act of 1854, which led to the establishment of the first reformatory schools to which children under sixteen could be sent at the end of their prison sentences.[30] A number of these schools were opened in London as well as a reformatory ship, the *Cornwall*, which was moored on the Thames in Essex. Children were not sent to a reformatory for their first offence but could be for a subsequent one. Those who were sent to a reformatory could expect a sentence of several years under a harsh regime with severe punishments, including beatings. The long sentences were intended to keep the offender away from his former associates and the environment which had led him into crime. There were separate reformatories for girls. Attention was then turned to children considered to be in danger of becoming criminals, who were referred to as 'the perishing classes'. Under a series of Industrial School Acts passed in the 1850s and 60s, magistrates received powers to send seven to fourteen-year-olds to industrial schools. Children sent to these institutions included beggars, orphans, the children of prisoners and those found to be associating with criminals. Both reformatory and industrial schools provided training in trades such as shoemaking and tailoring, and domestic skills to help inmates to find work on release.

With the introduction of reformatory and industrial schools children were made wards of the state for the first time. Their parents were henceforth held responsible for neglecting them and compelled to pay for their maintenance while in the care of the state or suffer other penalties for failing in their parental duty. The state now stepped in to supply the care, attention and guidance which these parents had failed to provide. As a result of this legislation, juvenile crime rates began to fall by the 1860s. Nevertheless, crime continued to be a way of life for some of London's street children and juvenile criminals remained a source of anxiety in the metropolis. They continued to be written about in the press and were the subject of much discussion and deliberation.

CHAPTER 7

Child Prostitutes

There is no country or city, or town, where this evil is so systematically, so openly, or so extensively carried on, as in England, and her chief city.

Report of Mr Talbot, Secretary to the London Society for the Prevention of Juvenile Prostitution, 1835

... Some of these girls are of a very tender age – from thirteen years and upwards. You see them wandering along Leicester Square, and about the Haymarket, Tichbourne Street, and Regent Street. Many of them are dressed in a light cotton or merino gown, and ill-suited crinoline, with light grey, or brown cloak, or mantle. Some with pork-pie hat, and waving feather – white, blue or red; others with a slouched straw-hat. Some of them walk with a timid look, others with effrontery. Some have a look of artless innocence and ingenuousness, others very pert, callous and artful. Some have good features and fine figures, others are coarse-looking and dumpy, their features and accent indicating that they are Irish cockneys. They prostitutes themselves for a lower price, and haunt those disreputable coffee-shops in the neighbourhood of the Haymarket and Leicester Square, where you may see the blinds drawn down, and the lights burning dimly within, with notices over the door that "beds are to be had within".

Henry Mayhew
London Labour and the London Poor, 1851

Another way for children to make a living on the streets of London during this period was by prostitution. Child prostitutes came from the same backgrounds as other street children and came in contact with them in the slum areas and common lodging houses. Prostitution, or the 'Great Social Evil' as it was referred to at the time, was an enormous and highly visible problem. In 1842 Flora Tristan wrote:

There are so many prostitutes in London that one sees them everywhere, at any time of day, the streets are full of them.[1]

It is difficult to get an accurate picture of the scale of the problem because there was no clear legal definition of a prostitute and only those known to the police appeared in their statistics. It is clear, however, that a large number of children worked as prostitutes in London. The age of consent was just twelve until 1871, when it was raised to thirteen. The fact that it was illegal to have sex with under-age girls did not seem to offer them much protection. There was a great demand for young girls, partly because they were less likely to be infected with venereal disease.

Prostitution was not, in itself, a criminal offence, although keeping a disorderly house was. Prostitution was, however, closely connected with crime, including drunk and disorderly behaviour, assault and theft. It shared many of the same underlying causes as crime. Prostitutes, including the young ones, often lived and associated with criminals and some were criminals themselves, as the following description of Henry Mayhew's illustrates:

Many of these young girls – some of them good-looking – cohabit with young pickpockets about Drury Lane, St Giles's, Gray's Inn Lane, Holborn, and other localities – young lads from fourteen to eighteen, groups of whom may be seen loitering about the Haymarket, and often speaking to them. Numbers of these girls are artful and adroit thieves. They follow persons into the dark by-streets of these localities, and are apt to pick his pockets, or they rifle his person when in the bedroom with him in low coffee-houses and brothels. Some of these girls come even from Pimlico, Waterloo Road, and distant parts of the metropolis, to share in the spoils of fast life in the Haymarket. They occasionally take watches, purses, pins and handkerchiefs from their silly dupes who go with them into those disreputable places, and frequently are not easily traced, as many of them are migratory in their character.[2]

Although prostitutes were to be seen all over the metropolis, certain areas were notorious for them. The Haymarket, Holborn and the Strand were well known for higher class prostitutes, particularly in and around theatres, casinos and other amusement places. Waterloo Road was another notorious haunt for prostitutes and people who lived off their earnings. The most violent, disreputable and diseased prostitutes were to be found in the slums of Whitechapel, Shadwell, Spitalfields and the riverside of the East End. There were many brothels in these areas to serve sailors on leave.

The main underlying cause of prostitution was poverty resulting from the scarcity of work. Many young prostitutes were not inherently bad characters but were forced into the work out of financial desperation. W. O'Daniel stated in 1859 that:

There is not a particle of doubt but that stern necessity makes more persons wicked than does the love of iniquity.[3]

Some girls went straight from the workhouse onto the streets. There was intense competition for jobs in domestic service, which was the only alternative option for them. Girls in low paid work, like millinery and seamstressing, were often forced to supplement their income by prostitution in order to survive. Henry Mayhew spoke to many girls in this position. The following account, related by a girl turned out onto the streets by her father, is typical of a number he heard.

> I've been out in the streets three years. I work at the boot-binding, but can't get a living at it ... If I get bread, sir, by my work, I can't get clothes. For the sake of clothes or food I'm obliged to go into the streets, and I'm out regularly now, and I've no other dependence at all but the streets. If I could only get an honest living, I would gladly leave the streets.[4]

Working as an amateur prostitute or 'dollymop' could be a source of easy money but girls of good character often had to fortify themselves with alcohol to earn it. Prostitution was a deliberate choice for some, being preferable in many ways to working in shops, sweat-shops, factories, domestic service or other street occupations. It took much longer in most other jobs to earn what a prostitute could earn in one night, and, as long as a girl remained independent of pimps and brothel owners, she had more freedom too. Prostitution was also more profitable than stealing. Sometimes it was only resorted to occasionally to earn extra money. The following statement of an abandoned and unemployed girl whom Mayhew met in an Asylum for the Houseless Poor illustrates how difficult it was to resist the temptation of resorting to prostitution:

> "After I lost my work, I made away with what little clothes I had, and now I have got nothing but what I stand upright in." (The tears were pouring down the cheeks of the poor girl; she was many minutes afterwards before she could answer my questions, from sobbing). "I can't help crying," she said," when I think how destitute I am. Oh, yes, indeed (she cried through her sobs,), I have been a good girl in all my trials. I might have been better off if I had chosen to take to that life. I need not have been here if I had chosen to part with my character."[5]

Some unfortunate girls were on the streets because they had run away from bad homes and cruel parents. Others, probably the saddest of all, were forced into prostitution by their parents or other adults. Fyodor Dostoevsky noticed how prostitutes brought their own daughters to the Haymarket and made them ply the same trade. He left the following disturbing description:

Little girls, aged about twelve, seize you by the arm and beg you to come with them. I remember once amidst the crowd of people in the street I saw a little girl, not older than six, all in rags, dirty, bare-foot and hollow-cheeked; she had been severely beaten, and her body, which showed through the rags, was covered with bruises ... But what struck me most was the look of such distress, such hopeless despair on her face that to see that tiny bit of humanity already bearing the imprint of all that evil and despair was somehow unnatural and terribly painful.[6]

Some young prostitutes were originally victims of seduction, including servants seduced by their masters. The plight of this group, in particular, was to become a focus of attention for those campaigning for government action on prostitution. W. O'Daniel described them as:

Originally seduced from a state of innocence, and then abandoned by everyone who held them in any degree of estimation, they are left upon the world, and have no alternative but to go on in the way they have commenced.[7]

Innocent young girls were also abducted and forced into prostitution. No girls were safe alone in the metropolis; they were picked up at railway stations, in parks and at factory gates. This wicked practice was known as 'trepanning'. Bracebridge Hemyng, one of Mayhew's collaborators, described what happened once an unprotected child was 'decoyed under some pretext' to a brothel.

No sooner is the unsuspecting helpless one within their grasp than, by a preconcerted measure, she becomes a victim to their inhuman designs. She is stripped of the apparel with which parental care or friendly solicitude had clothed her, and then, decked with the gaudy trappings of her shame, she is compelled to walk the streets, and in her turn, while producing to her master or mistress the wages of her prostitution, becomes the ensnarer of the youth of the other sex.[8]

Once trapped, there was no escape for these children. The same fate awaited those tricked by bogus employment bureaux into prostitution.

The moral depravity of the low lodging houses, where people were herded together indiscriminately and bed sharing between strangers was common, was another cause of juvenile prostitution. Girls from poor, but good, families forced to lodge in such places were also vulnerable. Men picked up in the streets were taken back to lodging houses. Prostitution was also a logical progression from promiscuity, which was widespread among girls of the London underclass. The lewd entertainment in penny gaffs and music halls, so enjoyed by the juvenile poor, were also blamed for encouraging prostitution.

A true story related by Charles Dickens provides a good illustration of the step-by-step journey of young girls towards prostitution. Although the events related occurred in 1835, many young girls followed a similar path in the Victorian period. A curious Dickens joined a crowd of people who were watching newly convicted prisoners being collected by a police van outside Bow Street police station. The first prisoners, handcuffed together, were sisters aged about sixteen and fourteen. Although their gaudy clothes revealed that they were prostitutes, it was not clear what offences they had been convicted of. Dickens was struck by the complete contrast in the demeanour of the two girls. The younger one was:

> ... weeping bitterly – not for display, or in the hope of producing effect, but for very shame; her face was buried in her handkerchief: and her whole manner was but too expressive of bitter and unavailing sorrow.[9]

For the older girl, who had been sentenced to six months and labour, this was obviously not a new experience. She cheekily ordered the coachman to drop her off 'in Cold Bath Fields – large house with a high garden-wall in front; you can't mistake it.'[10]

The younger sister had just received her first conviction, which accounted for her shame and distress. Dickens observed that:

> These two girls had been thrown upon London streets, their vices and debauchery, by a sordid and rapacious mother. What the younger girl was then, the elder had been once; and what the elder then was, the younger must soon become. A melancholy prospect, but how surely to be realized; a tragic drama, but how often acted![11]

Dickens predicted a dire future for these girls and the countless others like them.

> Step by step, how many wretched females, within the sphere of every man's observation, have become involved in a career of vice, frightful to contemplate; hopeless at its commencement, loathsome and repulsive in its course; friendless, forlorn and unpitied, at its miserable conclusion.[12]

The future for a number of London's juvenile prostitutes in the early to mid-Victorian period was, indeed, bleak. Some died young on 'foul wards' or in 'lock hospital', where those infected with venereal disease were treated, or alone on the streets, having been discarded by brothel keepers. Others went on to become hardened adult prostitutes. A few were rescued by charities and societies set up to help them. For the majority, however, prostitution was fortunately a transitory phase and they moved on to a better life. This often included marriage or cohabitation, as an early career in vice did not matter in a social class which did not value virginity.

Throughout this period prostitution was widely regarded as a great, but necessary, social evil. As with other social issues, the attitude of successive governments was to leave well alone. They did not want to interfere with the liberty of the subject and were loath, therefore, to attempt to control prostitution. Eventually, following growing concern, particularly in the press and among the clergy, a government inquiry into prostitution was ordered. This was carried out by William Acton, a doctor and writer on medical matters. *Prostitution Considered in its Moral, Social and Sanitary Aspects in London and Other Large Cities and Garrison Towns* was published in 1853. Acton called for prostitution to be officially recognised so that its causes could be remedied and resulting evils checked, both for the sake of society and prostitutes themselves. However, most of his recommendations were ignored. The only legislation passed as a result of Acton's report was a series of Contagious Diseases Acts to protect the men who used prostitutes. Nothing was done by the government to help the many children who worked as prostitutes or to deal with the social problems which forced them into such a dangerous occupation.

The middle classes turned a blind eye to prostitution at this time, even though it offended their ideals of cleanliness and purity. It was condoned in a way in which crime was not. This was because so many men from the better-off classes, demonstrating the double standards of the day, used prostitutes themselves. The wives and daughters of these men, meanwhile, lived the saintly, sheltered lives of the middle-class Victorian 'angel in the house'. Prostitution was seen mainly as a physical and moral threat to the health and well-being of the nation. There was very little concern for the plight of prostitutes, including children. This was another example of Victorian indifference to the suffering of poor children. The only sympathy for these children was shown by religiously motivated people such as those who set up 'The London Society for the Protection of Young Females and the Prevention of Juvenile Prostitution' in 1835.

The findings of the social investigative journalists on prostitution in London must have been a real jolt to the complacency of their middle-class readers. They provided facts and figures as well as emphasising the link between prostitution and the feared feral underclass. It is difficult to imagine even the most hard-hearted person remaining unmoved by some of their graphic revelations. Henry Mayhew, Thomas Archer and Charles Dickens were all very concerned about the plight of child prostitutes. Mayhew was so moved by their suffering that he made little comment on the first-hand accounts of child prostitution which he recorded, except to blame a society which allowed such a state of affairs to exist but did nothing to remedy its causes. In his letter to *The Morning Chronicle* dated 13 November 1849 he wrote:

The facts that I have to set before the public in my present communication are
of so awful and tragic a character that I shall not even attempt to comment upon

them. The miseries they reveal are so intense and overwhelming that, as with all deep emotions, they are beyond words.[13]

Thomas Archer wanted the middle classes to see what existed beyond the respectability of their own lives. He particularly wanted them to be aware of young child prostitutes 'with the evil eyes and dead debauched faces of those who grow quickly old in vice'.[14] Charles Dickens, as will be seen in the next chapter, channelled his anger into offering practical help to girls caught up in prostitution.

Child prostitutes, like other street children, were a blight on, and embarrassment to, London, especially as it was in the process of being transformed into a grand imperial capital. The co-existence of hideous brothels, where moral depravity and wicked exploitation flourished, with the beauty and elegance of the fine new buildings provided yet another example of the extreme contrasts to be found in Victorian London. This contrast must have been very noticeable to the many foreign visitors who encountered this seedy side of London life as they followed the tourist trail or enjoyed an evening out in the entertainment districts.

CHAPTER 8

A Place to Sleep: The Homes of the Street Children

The great mass of the metropolitan community are as ignorant of the destitution and distress which prevail in large districts of London ... as if the wretched creatures were living in the very centre of Africa.

James Grant
Lights and Shadows of London Life, 1842

It is to the arches of the railway – those great bare blank walls of brick which are sometimes supposed to have made a clean sweep in a whole neighbourhood of evil repute, but which in reality build the traffic of foot-passengers out of the slums which crouch behind them – that the homeless children go for shelter, happy if an empty van, a cart, a wagon, a pile of timber is lying there to keep them from the bitter wind. Is there a carpenter's shop, a smith's shop, a nook of brickwork, or any sort of projection that can hide a dog: there you may find a child for whom the law has done no more than to teach them that practically everybody is supposed to be guilty till he can prove himself innocent; and for whom the Gospel has done nothing, for he has heard no part of it. The glad tidings of greatest joy to him would be to learn where to find food, a fire and a bed this piercing night, without being "jawed at" and "knocked about", and treated like – well, no! there is a Society for the Prevention of Cruelty to Animals, which would protect the dog.

Thomas Archer
The Terrible Sights of London, 1870

The children who spent so much of their lives on the London streets at this time lived, or at least sought shelter in, many different places. These included slum tenements and jerry-built back-to-back houses, common lodging houses, night shelters, refuges, casual wards of the workhouse and, in the absence of any alternative, the streets themselves.

There had been slums in London for many centuries. Hogarth's paintings vividly portray the vile slums of Georgian times. Those of the Victorian era, however, were even worse. The older slums had generally been confined to the City area but, with the rapid and unprecedented increase in the capital's population, slums had grown up in all directions. As the City itself developed into a business and commercial centre, the shops moved to the West End. Houses in the City were demolished and replaced by offices, banks and commercial buildings. An exodus began from the City as the capital expanded. Those who could afford to live in the new suburbs and commute in to work by train or omnibus moved away from the centre. They included the working classes in regular employment who could afford the workmen's train fare. Those houses vacated by the better-off which were not demolished for redevelopment were rapidly taken over by the very poor. Dwellings which had once housed one family became grossly overcrowded slum homes, crammed from cellar to attic with the poorest of the poor.

Unscrupulous landlords crowded in as many people as possible. Large profits could be made out of London's poorest citizens, who needed to live near their work in the docks, in market places, on building sites or wherever there was the prospect of casual work. Those who scraped a living on the streets also needed to be in the centre of the capital.

Slum districts were located throughout the metropolis. The most notorious included Seven Dials and Saffron Hill near Holborn, Bedfordbury near Covent Garden, Pye Street near Westminster Abbey, Ratcliff Highway in the East End and Jacob's Island in Bermondsey, south of the river. There were numerous other slums, less well known but equally appalling. As John Hollingshead pointed out in *Ragged London in 1861*, many of these areas were only known to 'the hard working clergy, certain medical practitioners and a few parochial officers'.[1]

Victorian slums were known as 'rookeries' because the inhabitants were all crammed together in colonies like rooks in nests. Families often had to sub-let to pay their rent and ten or more people to a room was common. There are numerous contemporary descriptions of these slums written by journalists, the clergy, mission and charity workers, and foreign visitors. The last named were particularly shocked at the conditions in which the poorest citizens of the world's richest capital were allowed to live. One such foreign visitor was Flora Tristan, whose journal contains a record of her trip to London in 1839. She visited a slum area inhabited by Irish immigrants which was located roughly where Charing Cross Road, Shaftesbury Avenue and New Oxford Street are today. Little Dublin, as this area was called, was reached by a dark, narrow alley off Tottenham Court Road. Within yards of what Tristan described as the 'elegant thoroughfare of Oxford Street with its throng of carriages; its wide pavement and splendid shops'[2] existed the most appalling slums imaginable. They were part of the notorious St Giles' parish. Tristan recorded her fear as she approached the area and the 'poisonous smell' which instantly hit her.

We turned off to the right into another unpaved, muddy alley with evil smelling soapy water and other household slops even more fetid lying elsewhere in stagnant pools. I had to struggle in revulsion and summon up all my courage to go on through this veritable cesspool. In St Giles the atmosphere is stifling, there is no fresh air to breathe, no daylight to guide your steps.[3]

Flora Tristan was staggered at the sight of 'such extreme poverty, such total degradation'. She was more shocked by the sight of the bedraggled and barefoot inhabitants of these slums, including many children, than the dreadful conditions in which they lived.

All this is horrifying enough, but it is nothing compared with the expressions of the people's faces. They are all fearfully thin, emaciated and sickly; their faces, necks and hands are covered with sores; their skin is so filthy and their hair so matted and dishevelled that they look like negroes; their sunken eyes express a stupid animal ferocity, but if you look at them with assurance they cringe and whine.[4]

The tiny children, either naked or wearing just a torn shirt, were especially pitiable. Children such as these, who already spent most of their time on the streets of the slums, were very likely in a few years to become the worst kind of street children. Flora Tristan was outraged at the appalling contrast between the lives of the rich and the poor in London. The motivation for publishing her journal was to reveal the dreadful human suffering on which the wealth and luxury of the world's richest capital was based.

George Godwin recorded the findings of his investigations of the slums in *London Shadows, A Glance at the 'Homes' of the Thousands,* published in 1854. As a builder, he was particularly interested in the structure and condition of the slum houses. The following is his description of housing in Clerkenwell, close to the foully polluted River Fleet.

Few would suppose that these dilapidated buildings were inhabited, and that too in the midst of winter, by human beings. In some parts the glass and framing (of the windows) have been entirely removed, and vain attempts made to stop out the wind and snow by sacking and other matter. The basement is occupied by donkeys and dogs ... There was no bedstead or other furniture in the room; the ceiling was cracked and rotten, and the window destroyed.[5]

Ironically, many of these streets had such attractive names as Rose Alley and Pear Tree Court.

It was in the courts and alleys of the slum districts that another group of street children could be seen. These were the 'little mothers', older children, usually girls, who had to take on the responsibility of looking after younger siblings while their parents worked, or to help their over-burdened mothers. Some looked after the young children and babies of neighbours for a few pennies a week. They spent their days nursing babies and watching over little children as they played in the filthy gutters. Like so many other street children, the 'little mothers' were forced to grow up before their time because of the adult responsibilities they were compelled to assume.

The terrible conditions recorded by Tristan and Godwin would have fitted any one of the numerous metropolitan slums. It is no wonder that the very poor suffered so badly in the regular outbreaks of typhoid and cholera which earned London the title 'the capital of cholera'. Overcrowded run-down housing, an absence of clean, fresh water and sanitation, refuse and sewage filled streets and a poor diet made slum dwellers extremely vulnerable to contagious diseases. It is not surprising that Henry Mayhew, knowing the home environment in which many street children were reared, was so concerned about their physical, moral and spiritual welfare. The virtues of cleanliness, godliness, thriftiness and sobriety, so dear to the Victorian middle class, had no chance of existing in such homes. In nearly every slum street there were public houses and gin shops where the poor regularly wasted scarce money in drowning their sorrows. Children were frequently found inside these sordid places too – selling fruit and nuts, buying jugs of beer or retrieving drunken parents.

Incredibly, conditions in the slums of the metropolis got worse as London was modernised. The new transport infrastructure required to cope with the expanding capital and its exploding population led to the displacement of vast numbers of the poor as slums were demolished for road widening and railway construction. Thirty-seven thousand were believed to have been displaced by the railways alone between 1857 and 1869.[6] During this process no provision was made for those who lost their homes. Thus, ever more people were crammed into the remaining slum homes and conditions deteriorated still further. Instances of up to forty people living in one room were recorded. Caught up in this hideous social evil were many of the children who were to be seen at all hours of the day and night on the streets of the capital.

Limited government attempts during this period to improve the metropolitan slums had little effect. The General Sanitation Act of 1865 was an attempt to force landlords to improve the sanitary condition of their properties but it failed due to widespread non-enforcement. The Torrens Act of 1868 was intended to compel property owners to maintain rented accommodation in good repair but for various reasons turned out to be ineffective and made little difference.[7] The only action that appears to have been taken by landlords was to take advantage of increased demand for accommodation by raising rents.

The abject poor, most of whom were casual workers or unemployed, did not benefit from action taken to provide better housing for the working classes. The

Metropolitan Act for Improving Dwellings of the Industrious Classes, passed in 1841, and the Artisans and Labourers' Dwellings Act of 1867 only helped the honest and industrious 'deserving poor'. The 'undeserving poor' were also precluded from the help of such charitable institutions as the Metropolitan Association for Improving the Conditions of the Labouring Classes. The very poorest were unable to afford the rents of the new barrack-style blocks of model dwellings built by philanthropists such as Octavia Hill and George Peabody. They would also have struggled to comply with the conditions and rules imposed on tenants to enforce cleanliness, order and good behaviour. The poorest slum dwellers, including some street children, had no alternative therefore but to continue to endure the foul living conditions to which they were accustomed.

Another evil to be found in the slum districts were the common lodging houses. Often called 'low lodging houses' in acknowledgement of their degradation, they were located in all parts of the metropolis but certain districts were notorious for them. These included the parish of St Giles in central London, Rosemary Lane near the Tower of London, Thrald Street in Whitechapel and the streets near the East End docks. These doss-houses were as overcrowded, dilapidated, dirty and insanitary as the slum homes surrounding them; most had no privies or fresh water at all. For 2d a night the homeless could share, usually with total strangers, a filthy, verminous bed in a foul-smelling, unventilated, mixed sex room, with the use of a fire to cook on thrown in. For those who could only afford a penny there was just a heap of rags on a cold floor. Not surprisingly, contagious diseases were rife in lodging houses. Street children stayed in these ghastly hovels alone, with comrades or with their family if they had one. It does not take much imagination to work out the moral as well as the physical dangers these children were exposed to.

Mayhew recorded a description of a typical lodging house in the words of a man who had to stay in one after losing his job and being reduced to 'utter want'.

> I myself have slept in the top room of a house not far from Drury Lane, and you could study the stars, if you were so minded, through the holes left by the slates having been blown off the roof. It was a fine summer's night, and the openings in the roof were then rather an advantage, for they admitted air, and the room wasn't so foul as it might have been without them. I never went there again, but you may judge what thoughts went through a man's mind – a man who had seen prosperous days – as he lay in a place like that, without being able to sleep, watching the sky.[8]

This man had collected 'a handful of bugs' from the bedclothes. He reported that rooms in such lodging houses were regularly so crammed with sleepers 'that their breaths in the dead of night and in the unventilated chamber, rose … in one foul, choking steam of stench.'[9] Lodging houses were used by sailors, market porters, dock and building workers, job seekers, vagrants, beggars, pickpockets and minor criminals. The worst establishments, those haunted by prostitutes and hardened criminals, were dens of iniquity and immorality. Many lodging house landlords acted as fences for stolen goods. As Mayhew pointed out, any child fortunate enough to have received moral training from their parents had no chance of practising it if they were forced to find shelter in low lodging houses.

Lord Shaftesbury succeeded in getting two acts through Parliament in 1851 to improve common lodging houses used by 'transients'. Registration and inspection by the police to ensure cleanliness and end overcrowding became compulsory. These acts led to the closure of the worst thief houses and some improvements generally.[10] The street children who used lodging houses were among those who benefited from this.

In 1845, Friedrich Engels estimated that 50,000 people in London got up every morning not knowing where they would sleep that night.[11] This number would have included numerous street children. One place in which these children sought a bed for the night, often alone, was in a charity-run 'House of Refuge for the Destitute Poor', also known as 'straw-yards'. These shelters, which were only opened in the most severe winter weather, provided food, washing facilities and a place to sleep. Henry Mayhew described a visit to the refuge in Playhouse Yard, Cripplegate, in a letter published in *The Morning Chronicle* in January 1850. Housed in a former hat factory, this shelter was opened in 1820 by 'the benevolent founder Mr Hick, the city mace-bearer.'[12] Mayhew observed the motley assortment of desperate people waiting outside the refuge.

> The doors open into a narrow by-street, and the neighbourhood needs no other announcement that the establishment is open for the reception of the houseless, than the assembly of a crowd of ragged shivering people, certain to be seen on the night of opening, as if they knew by instinct where they might be housed under a warm and comfortable roof. The crowd gathers in Playhouse -yard, and many among them look sad and weary enough. Many of the women carry infants at the breast, and have children by their sides holding by their gowns. The cries of these, and the wrangling of the hungry crowds for their places, is indeed disheartening to hear.[13]

At five o'clock an officer stepped out and admitted two hundred people. Those with tickets from previous nights were allowed in first. Newcomers were given tickets for three nights' lodgings. Those let in were first led away to wash and to undergo a thorough medical examination. Pregnant women and anyone with a contagious disease or skin disorder were segregated. These people were not rejected but were provided with alternative accommodation. Mayhew noticed how everyone was treated kindly and with respect and how lively and merry many of the young street boys were, compared with the others who had been admitted. They were clearly relieved at the prospect of a brief respite from their brutal existence and food to ease their hunger.

A description of those admitted with details of their age, trade and parish of origin were entered in a large ledger. Each one, including the tiniest baby, was given gruel, half a pound of best bread and unlimited water. They slept in coffin-like beds, on a hay mattress with a sheepskin cover. The building, which had a 'warm and cosy feel', was immaculately clean. Further rations were handed out as people left the following morning. Unfortunately, there were not enough of these refuges to help more than a few of those in need for a brief period in the worst weather; most of those who sought shelter had to be turned away. Many people, including children, must have perished after failing to gain admittance to a night refuge. Admirable though these charitable efforts were, they were totally inadequate in the face of London's overwhelming and widespread poverty.

In the early to mid-Victorian period the only shelter for the homeless and destitute which was not provided by charity was the workhouse. Long-term shelter was provided in the workhouse itself and temporary shelter in the casual ward, which was usually housed in the same building or close by. The horrors of the Victorian workhouse are well known. Under the Poor Law Amendment Act of 1834 parishes which had previously supported one workhouse were joined together in unions, with one large workhouse per union. These grim, forbidding buildings, similar in appearance to prisons, were popularly known as 'bastilles'. A Board of Guardians, elected by local ratepayers and answerable to a central Poor Law Commission, managed the new workhouses. The Guardians were also accountable to the ratepayers and came under pressure to keep the cost of the new system down. The old system of outdoor relief was abolished. The new Poor Law was intended to force people to protect themselves against unemployment, sickness and the death of the family breadwinner, and not to rely on the state. The only relief available after 1834 was, therefore, inside the workhouse, where conditions were made deliberately harsh to make them less attractive, or 'less eligible', than those under which the lowest paid worker outside existed. Any able-bodied person who entered a workhouse had to 'work' in return for relief in order to deter the idle and work-shy and instil a work ethic. However, the new system failed to make allowances for the fact that some people were too sick, old or frail to work, that there were not enough jobs to go round and that much employment suitable for the unskilled was casual or seasonal.

London workhouses were under much greater pressure than those in the rest of the country because of the peculiar circumstances which prevailed in the capital. London really needed its own system of poor relief, tailored to its particular needs.[14] The rapidly increasing population included a large number of vagrants and the pull factors which continued to draw people to the metropolis created intense pressure on its workhouses. This increased considerably during periods of economic depression and in harsh winters. The cost of poor relief in London doubled between 1851 and 1869. It had proved impossible to abolish outdoor relief in the capital completely, even for the able-bodied, as required under the 1834 Act, because of the overwhelming level of need.[15] A description by James Grant of the dispensation of outdoor relief, in the form of bread, to a crowd outside a London workhouse in 1838 indicates how desperately this help was still needed. Grant was shocked at the 'overbearing and outrageous manner' of the officials handing out this meagre relief to the abject poor.

> A more miserable group of human beings I have never seen; a more wretched assemblage, judging from their outward appearance, I should suppose, are but seldom to be witnessed in any civilised country. When one succeeded in getting a loaf, every eye was directed to it in a moment, with an eagerness and intensity of gaze which told much more forcibly than words could, the hunger which the poor creatures were enduring. The eyes of the children looked with a specially expressive gaze at the article of food. But what was most eloquent and affecting of all, as showing the agony which the poor young creatures were suffering from want of food, was the almost ferocious-like manner in which they seized the loaf, the moment their mothers got one, and the ravenous voracity with which they began to eat it.[16]

The severe winter of 1860 to 1861 and the accompanying trade depression so exacerbated the already dire problem of poverty in London, especially in the East End, that the government was finally compelled to act.[17] Following a review of the administration of the Poor Law, the Metropolitan Houseless Poor Act of 1864 was passed, which extended the existing provision for 'destitute wayfarers, wanderers and foundlings', including able-bodied men who had previously been excluded. Conditions in the casual wards were deliberately grim and unwelcoming, and using them meant having to mix with habitual vagrants, criminals and other undesirables. In this respect they were much worse than the 'straw yards'. Some people travelled from one union casual ward to another, begging along the way. Street children used casual wards as a place to obtain an occasional brief respite and get their strength back before returning to the streets. Despite their drawbacks, casual wards at least provided a bed and food which did not have to stolen or begged for.

Mayhew likened conditions in one of these wards to those of a 'well kept stable'.[18] Conditions varied from one casual ward to another. A less favourable description was recorded by James Greenwood, who spent a night in the casual ward of Lambeth Workhouse in 1866 to find out for himself what conditions were like. In *A Night in a Workhouse* he wrote:

> No language with which I am acquainted is capable of conveying an adequate conception of the spectacle I then encountered. Imagine a space of about thirty feet by thirty enclosed on three sides by a dingy white-washed wall, and roofed

with naked tiles which were furred with the damp and filth that reeked within. As for the fourth side of the shed, it was boarded in for (say) a third of its breadth; the remaining space being hung with flimsy canvas, in which was a gap two feet wide at top, widening to at least four feet at bottom. This far too airy shed was paved with stone, the flags so thickly encrusted with filth that I mistook it at first for a floor of natural earth ... At one glance my appalled vision took in thirty of them – thirty men and boys stretched upon shallow pallets which put only six inches of comfortable hay between them and the stony floor.[19]

Adults were required to do three hours work at the hand corn mill or breaking stones and children at picking oakum in return for food and shelter. This was intended as a 'test of destitution and industry'. However, with the vast increase in numbers and the 'different class' of applicants to the casual ward, this requirement sometimes had to be dispensed with in London.

The casual wards, like the night shelters, could not accommodate all who sought relief there. Every day many were turned away from casual wards because there was no space for them. In 1856, Charles Dickens wrote the following description of a group of destitute people who had failed to gain admittance to a casual ward in Whitechapel.

Crouched against the wall of the Workhouse, in the dark street, on the muddy pavement-stones, with the rain raining upon them, were five bundles of rags. They were motionless, and had no resemblance to the human form. Five great beehives, covered with rags – five dead bodies taken out of graves, tied neck and heels, and covered with rags – would have looked like those five bundles upon which the rain rained down in the public street.[20]

These five desperate people included two young sisters. A passer-by informed Dickens that he often saw as many as twenty-five people turned away from that particular casual ward. Dickens, disturbed and angry, gave each of these miserable souls a shilling for food and lodgings elsewhere.

Some of the street children had formerly lived in the long-term wards of workhouses and some ended up in them, having finally lost the battle to survive unaided. Seeking shelter in the workhouse was, however, the last resort of the truly desperate. Poor people preferred to suffer the most severe privations than submit to such degradation and shame. In the words of James Grant:

By many of the inmates, the workhouse is regarded as a sort of sepulchre in which they are entombed alive.[21]

Many, including children, must have died of cold and starvation on the streets rather than endure this humiliation.

Street children entering a workhouse immediately lost their freedom, one of the few attractions of street life. If they entered with their parents they were separated from them and any siblings of the opposite sex, although some contact was allowed. New entrants had their hair cropped and were made to wear rough uniforms. Living conditions were harsh, discipline was often brutal and the food was poor and inadequate. In return for this 'relief' inmates were forced to do pointless, repetitive work. Children were usually given the task of unpicking old hemp rope for re-use. This horrible job, known as 'picking oakum', left small hands sore and bleeding. As with the casual wards, one of the worst features of the workhouse for the honest destitute must have been having to mix with criminals, prostitutes and the depraved, who also sheltered there.

Orphaned and abandoned workhouse children risked being apprenticed out, although they were no longer taken to the industrial north to provide slaves for factories and there were very few climbing boys left at this time. Long-term child inmates received a rudimentary education in the workhouse school, or at a local elementary school, to help them break out of the cycle of poverty. Some also received industrial training for the same purpose.

Children were generally accepted by the Victorians as being less to blame for their poverty than adults but those who came under the control of cruel workhouse masters and mistresses found little sympathy. Some workhouses, run by more humane officials, were better regulated than others and had less severe regimes. Nevertheless, for many children, including some former street children, the long-term wards of London workhouses did indeed turn out to be their 'sepulchres'. This happened less frequently after 1867, when the government passed the Metropolitan Poor Act, which removed the sick poor from the workhouse and set up hospitals for their use in large boroughs. This Act was important because it signified an apparent softening in the government's attitude to the poor and destitute.

The only other place for the homeless London street children to sleep at this time was on the streets themselves. In warm summer weather this was not too bad a prospect. Some children, like the 'King' of the tumbling boy crossing sweepers, actually chose to sleep rough with their street pals in good weather, even when they had a home to return to. On wet nights and during the cold winter months, however, this was not such an attractive option. Street children often sought warmth and shelter during the evenings in the ragged schools located in the poor districts of London. Once these closed they had to find somewhere else to shelter and spend the night. They were to be found, often huddled together for warmth, in doorways, on roof tops, in railway stations, on coal barges, deep inside dust heaps and in carts, wagons and empty barrels. Market places, where many hungry children scavenged among the rotting food refuse, were also popular sleeping locations.

Arches provided good shelter. Many homeless children slept under railway arches, under the dry arches of bridges across the Thames and in the maze of arches under the Adelphi Terrace off the Strand. In 1870, Thomas Archer described how children were often seen sheltering beneath arches in *The Terrible Sights of London.*

> Late wayfarers crossing some of the bridges at night may come upon them suddenly in the act of looking over the parapet into the stream below, and noting the ragged patches of moonlight reflected in it from the rift in the driving bank of cloud. Something moves in the dim recess of the stone-work in which we stand, and, peering down, we see a moving form, the gleam of a white limb amidst a mass of tatters. It is difficult to distinguish whether it is a human form or not, and yet there are limbs too – many limbs. There are stealthy eyes looking out to see what new enemy has come to this refuge for the destitute. Two or three pairs of eyes, scowling, furtive, almost threatening, and with the dogged, hunted glare in them that is so sad to see. The owners of these eyes are huddled together to form a mutual shelter against the chill night air, and you had better pass on your way.[22]

Street children also slept in London's parks and open spaces. Hyde Park was a popular location and one boy was known to sleep inside a lawn roller there. Early in the morning, children were often seen washing in the Serpentine before starting another long day on the streets. Later on, while the street urchins were occupied elsewhere, other children gathered in the same parks with their nannies. These children were far more likely to be loved, protected, cared for, educated, have all their needs provided and to have the luxury of enjoying their childhood as a special period in their lives before the adult world beckoned. The fortunes and prospects of these two different classes of children could not have been more different.

The descriptions of Henry Mayhew and other writers of the appalling living conditions endured by London's abject poor added to existing concerns voiced in the 1840s. Middle-class readers were disturbed by graphic revelations about the filthy slums. The prevailing belief in the miasma theory, that disease was carried in the air by bad smells, made them fear for their own safety. They were also no doubt shocked by the descriptions of drunkenness, feral behaviour and moral depravity of the slum dwellers. Their anxieties were heightened by the language of exploration used to describe the visits made by journalists to the slums. These were depicted as frightening journeys into unknown territories peopled by wild savages.

CHAPTER 9

Helping the Street Children

Umbrellas to mend, and chairs to mend, and clocks to mend, are called in our streets daily. Who shall count up the numbers of thousands of children to mend, in and about those same streets, whose voice of ignorance cries aloud as the voice of wisdom once did, and is as little regarded; who go to pieces for the want of mending and die unrepaired!

'Boys To Mend'
Charles Dickens
Household Words, 11 September 1852

The plight of London's street children during this period was desperate but they were not without help. This was directed at the poor in general as well as specifically at needy children, including those on the streets. Help for the street children arose partly from a desire to assist and rescue them for their own sakes but also had the ulterior motive of clearing them from the streets to benefit society in general and to protect the reputation of London. Some of the rescue work was, therefore, driven by self-interest.[1]

These efforts were vital in view of the persistence of the government policy of 'laissez faire'. There had been little response to Lord Shaftesbury's attempts to get Parliament to do something about London's destitute juvenile population. Social problems continued to be dealt with by the government only when they became too urgent to ignore any longer, and very slowly even then, as illustrated by the issue of sanitary reform in London which dragged on throughout the 1840s and 50s.

The 'laissez faire' policy with regard to poverty was the logical extension of the belief that the poor were to blame for their own predicament. It was considered the responsibility of the poor to lift themselves out of poverty by finding work, and to improve their living conditions by acquiring better habits and morals. The solution was thought to lie in adopting the middle-class virtues of hard work, cleanliness, godliness, thriftiness and sobriety. It was not appreciated that a steady job and a decent home were essential before these virtues could be practised and that poverty was usually caused by circumstances beyond the control of its victims. It was some time before the full scale of problems such as unemployment and overcrowding, which resulted from the rapid urbanisation and expansion of London, became evident. Also, the realisation that London's extreme social problems needed different solutions to those of the rest of the country was slow to dawn.[2] The workhouse, the casual ward and the limited outdoor relief provided were totally inadequate, so those in need had to look elsewhere for help.

Street children, especially those who lived in the slums, were often helped by other poor people. Friends and neighbours came to each other's assistance in the poorest communities. Unlike the charity offered by other classes, such help was not officially recorded, although investigative journalists, the clergy and mission workers were aware of it. Henry Mayhew claimed that the help the poor gave to each other was greater than that provided by philanthropists. George Sims, author of *How the Poor Live,* described 'the charity which robs itself to give to others' is 'nowhere so common as among the poor.'[3]

The poor assisted each other both in times of difficulty and crisis, such as childbirth, illness, death and imprisonment, as well as on a day-to-day basis. Some street children benefited from such aid and it often made their lives easier. Abandoned, orphaned, abused and neglected children were frequently taken in by kindly kin and neighbours to save them from cruel parents and the workhouse. Henry Mayhew interviewed a number of children on the streets who had been given a home, even if only a share of a slum room, by aunts, grandparents, older siblings and neighbours. One such example was the two orphaned flower girls and their brother who were looked after by their caring landlady. Sometimes such kindness saved children from the streets or, at the very least, provided shelter and adult support. No doubt in some cases this kind of help rescued children from descending into crime and prostitution and even made the difference between life and death.

Despite the prevailing belief that the poor were the authors of their own misfortune, the better-off classes who were aware of their plight were not indifferent to their suffering. Throughout the nineteenth century there was a flood of compassion and charity for a wide range of people in need and distress in London. Those in a position to help and inclined to do so were generous with their time, money and talents. As one journalist commented, 'The facility with which money can be raised in London for charitable purposes is very astonishing'.[4] *The Charities of London in 1852–3,* a contemporary book by Sampson Low, listed a total of 530 charitable institutions and societies in the metropolis, the majority of which were established before the revelations of the social investigative journalists. This list included seventeen institutions for reclaiming fallen women, thirteen for the relief of street destitution and distress, one hundred and twenty-six charities for the elderly, nine for the blind, deaf and dumb, thirteen asylums for orphans, fifteen for other children and forty-three home mission societies. Charitable funds came from donations, legacies, subscriptions, church collections and fund-raising events.

Despite the great outpouring of help for the needy and distressed, many of London's better-off citizens did not know about the conditions in which the poor lived. Once they were enlightened by the social investigative journalists, many middle-class people offered financial help. A number of Mayhew's readers responded to his plea 'to lay to heart' his revelations and take up the cause of the poor by sending donations for the people he wrote about. Mayhew, like many of his fellow journalists and writers, disagreed with what was termed 'indiscriminate' or 'mistaken' charity. They preferred help that would enable the poor to help themselves. Mayhew was against the dispensing of alms because he believed that 'the most dangerous lesson that can possibly be taught to any body of people whatsoever is that there are other ways of obtaining money than by working for it.'[5] He insisted that the donations he received were used to set up a 'Loan Office for the Poor' under the control of his publisher. Those deemed deserving enough were allowed small grants or cheap loans on easy terms from the fund to buy stock or equipment to set themselves up in, or continue, a trade. Some street children could well have benefited from this fund. It is difficult to tell the extent of the help offered by readers moved by Mayhew's articles. Having salved their middle-class consciences by making donations, many probably carried on with their lives and did no more. However, they may equally have contributed to a further increase in the number of charities established throughout this period. By 1861, the number of London charities rose to 640.[6]

Much of the charity work in nineteenth-century London was carried out by evangelical Christians who were motivated by their religious beliefs. These philanthropists worked to relieve the physical distress and save the souls of the poor, hoping to secure their own salvation and demonstrate their love for their fellow men in the process. Some of the greatest philanthropists who used their wealth, talent and influence to help the London poor came from an evangelical background. Henry Mayhew was always suspicious of these philanthropists and mistrusted their motives. He was concerned that their efforts proceeded 'rather from a love of power than from a sincere regard for the people.'[7]

Anthony Ashley-Cooper, 7th Earl of Shaftesbury, was one of the most successful and well-known evangelical philanthropists of the period. He spent much of his life working for the poor and needy, especially children. It was through his perseverance and efforts that the sufferings of boy chimney sweeps came to an end. He also fought tenaciously, against vested interests, to improve the lives of children working for long hours in appalling conditions in England's mines and factories. Shaftesbury had a paternalistic belief that it was the duty of the higher classes to help their social inferiors and that the government should intervene to protect the weak and oppressed. He put pressure on successive governments to pass legislation to help the poor in various ways. It was Shaftesbury who first alerted the government in 1848 to the plight of London's destitute children and was actively involved in helping them throughout his long life.

Angela Burdett-Coutts was another philanthropist who made a considerable impact on the lives of the London poor. She spent the vast wealth she inherited from her grandfather, Thomas Coutts the banker, on a wide range of worthy causes. Burdett-Coutts was influenced by her father, the radical MP Francis Burdett, and was driven by a strong social conscience. She was described by the journalist Blanchard Jerrold as 'The Lady Bountiful of our time – at once wise, and gentle and charitable.'[8] The street children benefited from a number of the charities which Burdett-Coutts funded and helped, including the building of Columbia Market in Bethnal Green to provide good, cheap food for the poor, the work of the Ragged School Union, the founding of training ships to prepare destitute boys for the navy, the founding of a refuge for prostitutes and, later in the century, the establishment of the NSPCC.

Both men and women were involved in charity work among the London poor but the latter were particularly active. These women were largely from the middle class but a few were from lower down the social scale. Middle-class women had time on their hands because they were not permitted to do paid work outside the home and their role within the home was largely supervisory, with servants doing the domestic chores and caring for their children. The supposedly 'feminine' qualities of sympathy, compassion, patience, gentleness, humility, tact and self-sacrifice which so fitted them to be 'angels in the house' also fitted them to be 'angels out of the house'. Their organisational and supervisory skills were also useful in the philanthropic sphere. Furthermore, their responsibility for the moral and spiritual teaching of children and servants gave them the experience necessary to teach the gospel and all-important middle-class values to the poor. Philanthropic work gave middle-class women a fulfilling and important role improving society and helping the poor outside the narrow confines of their homes.[9]

Women founded and ran a wide variety of charitable societies and institutions for adults and children. They also raised funds and made personal donations. One very important area of their work was visiting the poor in their homes, either independently or as members of visiting societies. They went into some of the worst London slums, often in pairs for safety, to provide practical help and spiritual comfort. Their efforts were often greeted with hostility. Female charity workers also visited the poor in orphanages, infirmaries, refuges, reformatories, asylums and the workhouse. The street children were among the beneficiaries of such work.

The clergy of all denominations had been involved in relieving the distress of the metropolitan poor long before attention was drawn to their plight by journalists. A large part of their work involved ministering to slum dwellers in their homes, despite the fact that the majority of the poorest classes never set foot in a church.

Some clergymen, including Thomas Archer, wrote about their pastoral work among the poor in articles and books and thus added their voice to that of the journalists. Members of church visiting societies supported the clergy in their work. With 250 parish churches and 100 Episcopalian chapels in London, this added up to a considerable effort on behalf of the poorest and neediest.

Evangelical missions also made a huge contribution to the alleviation of poverty in London. Some, such as the Bethnal Green Mission, established in 1866 by Annie McPherson, a friend of Dr Barnardo, were small concerns. On a much larger scale was the work of the London City Mission, founded in 1835 by a group of people from different Protestant denominations. The mission recruited full-time paid male missionaries to go from door to door visiting residents. Their instructions were to bring Londoners, especially the poor, to Christ as well as 'do them good by every means in your power.'[10] They provided a wide range of practical help and became directly involved in the lives and problems of the poor. Like many other charity workers, they encouraged self-help and taught respectable middle-class values. The missionaries, of whom there were 275 across London by 1852,[11] were assisted by female volunteers. Despite frequent abuse and violence, these determined missionaries persevered and came to be accepted and respected friends of the poor. It was the London City Missionaries who first discovered the full extent of child destitution in the metropolis. As well as visiting the poor, the Mission laid on religious services, ragged schools, adult education classes, sewing meetings, excursions and temperance entertainment. The street children benefited from the Mission's work directed specifically at children as well as help received by their families. Lord Shaftesbury said he knew of no other mission 'doing such a widespread and efficacious work'.[12]

The Salvation Army also began its work among the London poor around this time. In 1865 William and Catherine Booth set up the Whitechapel Christian Mission. Both were committed social reformers as well as powerful and fervent preachers. The Mission became the Salvation Army in the later Victorian period, when it had its greatest impact.

Help and shelter were available to the street children in a number of refuges across the metropolis for the poor of all ages. Some refuges, however, only took in children who were accompanied by their mothers. Twenty-nine institutions which offered some kind of relief to street children were included in Low's List of Charities for 1852–3. One of the largest refuges in London was the Field Lane Refuge, which grew out of the Field Lane Ragged School. It was located in an area once notorious for thieves. The institution outgrew its original buildings and in 1865 Lord Shaftesbury laid the foundation of new premises in Saffron Hill. With an emphasis on self help, it provided food, shelter, baths and wash-houses, clothing clubs, savings banks, education, training and help in finding work as well as a shelter for those recently discharged from hospital. Around 10,000 adults and children shared in the benefits of this institution every year. In 1860 boys offered three nights a week respite from the streets numbered between seventy and two hundred per night and girls between thirty and one hundred.[13]

There were a number of orphanages founded by philanthropists and charities in London at this time but most only accepted children from respectable families. One such was the London Orphan Asylum in Clapton, whose inmates came from a background of 'genteel poverty'. Other orphanages only accepted children with a particular connection, such as the Soldiers' Daughters Home, The Merchant Seaman's Orphan Asylum and The Royal Caledonian Orphan Asylum. The vast majority of the street children were, therefore, excluded from seeking help from these and similar institutions.

Some orphanages and refuges for children did accept the very poor and would not have turned away a destitute child if they had enough room. Orphanages of this kind included the Alexandra Asylum, situated not far from Westminster Bridge, which took in deserted and orphaned girls to save them from prostitution, and the London Refuge for Homeless and Destitute Children. The latter was one of the largest refuges in London with a boys' home in Queen Street, Bloomsbury, and a girls' home in Broad Street. It was funded by voluntary contributions and profits from the sale of items made by the children. The only condition for admittance was destitution and the refuge was advertised by picture posters displayed in casual wards and other appropriate places. The children were fed, clothed, housed, educated and trained for work. They were taught to be self-sufficient by making their own shoes and clothing and doing their own laundry.

Thomas Archer visited the boys' refuge and was impressed, finding the place 'rough and ready'[14] but comfortable and welcoming. He remarked on the happy, industrious atmosphere and the children's 'healthy appetite for work'.[15] There were two branches of this refuge in the country; a 'retreat' for girls in Ealing and a farm school for boys in Woking. The various branches housed and helped several hundred children in all and the refectory in the boys' refuge was also opened up once a week to 500 more homeless boys. In 1866, under the direction of Lord Shaftesbury, an old ship was fitted out and used as a training ship to prepare 150 boys from the refuge for a life at sea. Other children were trained and sent out to the colonies to start a new life.

Much good work, supported by charitable donations and fund raising, was done to shelter and help London's homeless and destitute children. Such efforts, however, were nowhere near enough to cope with this vast problem. There was an urgent need for further provision on a larger scale. In the 1860s three men, motivated by their religious beliefs, sought to meet this need. The most famous of these was Thomas Barnardo, an evangelical Christian who came to London from Dublin in 1866 to train as a missionary and doctor with the intention of working for Dr Hudson's medical mission to China. Barnardo lived among the East End poor while he trained at the London Hospital in Whitechapel. He soon came face to face with extreme poverty and suffering while visiting the sick and dying during London's last cholera epidemic. Barnardo's work with poor children began when he became superintendent of a ragged school in Ernest Street, Mile End. In 1868 he founded the East End Juvenile Mission, which provided Bible classes, religious services, evening schools, industrial workshops and work in shoe-black brigades. Self-help was encouraged as the children who attended the mission had to work in return for food and clothing.

One cold night during the winter of 1869–70 a boy named Jim Jarvis was reluctant to leave the warmth of the evening school classroom after one of Barnardo's lessons. Barnardo was shocked to find out that the boy had no parents or home to return to and that he slept on the streets. The doctor had assumed that all the boys he helped had homes of some sort, even if only a room in a slum tenement or a shared bed in a common lodging house. Jim offered to show his teacher where he usually slept and led him to a roof top in Petticoat Lane Market where a group of boys were huddled together asleep. Barnardo learned that vast numbers of boys slept rough in London every night.

Following this shocking discovery, Dr Barnardo opened his first children's home in Stepney Causeway in 1870 and began his crusade to save the bodies and souls of London's street children. He went out on regular night searches to rescue homeless boys, taking Lord Shaftesbury with him on one occasion. On discovering seventy-three boys sleeping in the open at Billingsgate Market, Shaftesbury's appalled response was 'All London shall know of this!'[16] Dr Barnardo was offered help by Shaftesbury and other influential people, leading him to give up his ambition of becoming a medical missionary to concentrate all his efforts on helping the street children of the metropolis.

As well as housing and feeding the boys he rescued, Dr Barnardo provided them with a basic education, including moral and spiritual instruction. They were subjected to an organised and disciplined regime, were given work chopping and selling wood, as members of a messengers' brigade, as brush and toolmakers and in a 'tract' department producing and selling improving literature. All profits were used to run the home. The boys were, therefore, not only kept off the streets and out of trouble, but taught respectable Victorian middle-class values as well. By 1870 Dr Barnardo had made an impressive start on his crusade to save the street children.

Around the same time, Charles Haddon Spurgeon, the famous Baptist preacher, was offered £20,000 to build an orphanage for poor, fatherless boys. He was given the money after publishing an article on the need to increase the number of schools to teach the gospel to poor children. Thomas Archer visited his orphanage in Stockwell and reported its aspect as 'bright and cheerful, the air clear and salubrious.'[17] The education offered there was much wider than that usually considered sufficient for poor children and the ladies of his huge congregation gave regular gifts of food, clothing, bedding and toys. It is interesting to note that the Stockwell Orphanage was specifically for 'fatherless boys'. Some years earlier Henry Mayhew had revealed the particular problems suffered by widows left struggling on their own with a young family.

The third man who made a significant impact on the lives of London's destitute children, including many street children, was the Reverend Thomas Bowman Stephenson, a Methodist minister. In 1869, Stephenson and two Sunday school teachers converted a cottage near Waterloo Station into a home for boys; this was the beginning of the National Children's Home. Stephenson's mission statement was 'to rescue children who, through the death or vice or extreme poverty of their parents, are in danger of falling into criminal ways.'[18] His aims were the same as Barnardo's and Spurgeon's – to rescue children both physically and spiritually, to educate them and teach them discipline and to train them 'to industrious habits.'[19] All three men started by rescuing boys only, probably because the majority of 'street arabs' were boys. Despite their efforts, however, there were still countless children in London with nowhere to live but the streets.

Even if there had been enough orphanage places to accommodate all the destitute children, some would probably have chosen not to enter one. Their characteristic love of freedom, noted by Mayhew, would no doubt have led many of the more resilient children to prefer to take their chances on the streets. Some, like the members of the gang of crossing sweepers who worked in Trafalgar Square, were used to doing what they wanted and chose to take a day off work when they could afford to. Such boys would have missed the freedom of the streets and found the discipline and training imposed by orphanages too irksome.

Probably the most effective action taken on behalf of London's destitute children was the establishment, by individuals and charities, of ragged schools. The government's inadequate contribution to the education of London's destitute children was the building of five district or 'barrack' schools, each accommodating 1,000 pupils. There was, not surprisingly, some stigma attached to these Poor Law schools. Pauper children in the workhouse were provided with a rudimentary education or sent to a local state-aided school.

Ragged schools, therefore, met a desperate need. Such schools had existed in England since well before Victoria came to the throne in 1837. As their name suggests, these free schools were for children too poor, ragged, dirty, verminous and rough to be accepted by other schools, such as Sunday Schools and those run by the two state-aided voluntary religious societies. The founders of ragged schools were motivated by faith and compassion.

Many London ragged schools were started in makeshift buildings, such as old stables and filled-in railway arches, in the worst slum districts. Most were originally Sunday Schools which extended their hours to include week days and evenings. The teachers who ran the early schools were mainly untrained volunteers. They looked after the physical, moral and spiritual welfare of their pupils by providing a warm shelter, food, clothing and a rudimentary education with a high religious content. Treats and outings were often laid on too. Given the large classes and unruly behaviour many teachers had to contend with, it is debatable how much their pupils actually learned. Their most notable success was in civilizing their rough, uncouth and unmanageable charges. They also took large numbers of them off the streets and out of trouble for long periods, and provided them with the attention of concerned and dedicated adults.

Some ragged schools were small concerns, such as that founded by Quintin Hogg, a businessman, in Off Alley near the Strand in 1865. Hogg left the following description of his school.

> The class prospered amazingly; our little room which was only thirty foot long by twelve foot wide got so crammed that I used to divide the school into two sections of sixty each, the first lot coming from seven to eight-thirty, and the second lot from eight-thirty to ten. There I used to sit between two classes, perched on the back of a form, dining on my 'pint of thick and two doorsteps', as the boys used to call coffee and bread and treacle, taking one class in reading and the other at writing or arithmetic. Each section closed with a ten minutes' service and prayer.[20]

Other schools, such as those founded by the missionaries of the London City Mission, were part of a larger organisation. The Field Lane Ragged School, opened in 1841, became one of the largest in London. A description by Charles Dickens of the boys' class at this school is in marked contrast to the pleasant, orderly picture of the Off Alley school.

> The close, low, chamber at the back, in which the boys were crowded, was so foul and stifling as to be, at first, almost insupportable. But its moral aspect was so far worse than its physical, that this was soon forgotten. Huddled together on a bench about the room, and shown out by some flaring candles stuck against the walls, were a crowd of boys, varying from mere infants to young men; sellers of fruit, herbs, lucifer-matches, flints; sleepers under the dry arches of bridges; young thieves and beggars – with nothing natural to youth about them; with nothing frank, ingenuous, or pleasant in their faces; low-browed, vicious, cunning, wicked; abandoned of all help but this; – speeding downward to destruction, and UNUTTERABLY IGNORANT.[21]

The ragged school was the only hope for these boys and Dickens was encouraged by the efforts being made to help them. He noted that the work of civilising and inspiring hope in them had begun. Hopefully, these boys would have gone on to benefit from the other services offered by the large ragged schools such as hostels, industrial training and work opportunities.

In 1844, the Ragged School Union was established with Lord Shaftesbury as President, a position he held for forty years. The Union's object was to raise the profile of ragged schools, support their cause and to spread their 'humanising influence'. It also succeeded in drawing attention to the issue of educating the poor. In 1852 William Locke, Secretary to the Ragged School Union, reported to a Select Committee on Criminal and Destitute Children on the success of ragged schools. This committee was the government's response when it became clear that something needed to be done about London's street children. Locke reported that between 1844 and 1852 the number of ragged schools in London had risen from sixteen to 110. He gave a detailed description of the backgrounds of the pupils which tallied almost exactly with those of Mayhew's street children. Locke claimed that many pupils of previous bad character had been reformed and were doing well, including a number who had gone on to find good jobs at home and in the colonies. He pointed out that they dealt with the roughest children, often needing police help to control them, 'but it appears to me that nothing can withstand the influence of affection and kindness in that very debased class.'[22] By 1870 there were 191 ragged schools with over 32,000 pupils in London.[23] By that time pupils were taught by trained teachers and monitors as well as volunteers.

Charles Dickens, although a supporter of ragged schools, questioned their religious emphasis and saw them as a temporary stop-gap rather than a proper solution to the problem of destitute and criminal street children. Henry Mayhew, despite being in favour of educating the poor as a means of helping them to help themselves, doubted the effectiveness of ragged schools in reducing juvenile crime. In 1850 he argued his case in the pages of *The Morning Chronicle*, which led to a heated argument with the Ragged School Union.[24] His seemed a lone voice, however. Thomas Archer's view that ragged schools were 'a mighty power in this great city which had extended their benevolent influence throughout the poorest neighbourhoods'[25] was a more accurate reflection of contemporary opinion. When the ragged schools were made redundant, after the introduction of compulsory state education, the Ragged School Union became the Shaftesbury Society and continued to work for needy children.

A few charitable organisations existed in London to help criminal children, including the Royal Philanthropic Society established in 1790. The society founded an institution in Southwark to provide shelter for both boys and girls and train them to earn a living instead of begging and stealing. Work was found for the children and some emigrated to South Africa. In 1848, by which time the institution was helping boys only, it moved to Redhill in Surrey to get the children away from the temptations of London and into a healthier environment. There a farm school was established which by 1857 accommodated 250 boys. In 1861 the school became the Redhill Reformatory School and its emphasis changed from preventing boys from embarking on a life of crime to reforming those who had.[26]

Another institution was the School for Discipline in Paradise Road, Chelsea, established by Elizabeth Fry in 1825. It took in criminal girls aged from seven to thirteen who were sent by magistrates. The school provided them with another chance by training them as servants, finding work for them and following up their progress.

In 1856, the Reformatory and Refuge Union was formed 'to seek and save that which was lost'. It helped criminal children through its role in advising magistrates on the most appropriate school for individual children, pressing for the restriction of punishment for young criminals in reformatories and the setting up of special schools for the most difficult children. It also established 'half-way houses' for children released on special licence. In 1866 this charity appointed a Boys' Beadle to investigate the circumstances of children found on the streets of London and to return them to their parents, school, a place of safety, the police or a magistrate, as appropriate.[27]

In view of the government's 'laissez faire' attitude regarding prostitution, the only help available for prostitutes came from charities and philanthropic individuals. Since the eighteenth century there had been Magdalene institutions in London to rescue prostitutes, but they offered temporary help only, as inmates had to leave them after a year and invariably returned to the streets. The concern of the middle classes and evangelical Christians was reflected in the increase in refuges, societies and missions to rescue fallen women in the nineteenth century. Prostitution was seen largely as a moral issue and the emphasis was, therefore, on reclaiming women and girls from the streets and helping them to become respectable members of society again. Most were trained to become domestic servants. One refuge for fallen women was Urania House in Shepherd's Bush, founded by Charles Dickens and Angela Burdett-Coutts. This home was only for those deemed 'deserving' and its training emphasised the all-important middle-class values.

There were several refuges and societies in London which worked specifically with child prostitutes. The London Society for the Protection of Young Females and Prevention of Juvenile Prostitution, established in 1835, was one such society. In a transcript of the prosecution of a brothel owner instigated by the society, its objectives were described in the following words:

> The society did not attempt to grapple with the great mass of profligacy and delinquency which prevailed to so lamentable an extent in the metropolis, but confined its exertions to the rescue of those young girls, children of tender years, from the wretched scenes of vice and depravity which were momentarily to be met with in the houses of the description of which the defendant was accused of being the proprietor.[28]

One of the largest organisations was the Society for the Rescue of Young Women and Children, established in 1853. In its first eleven years it helped 3,940 young prostitutes by providing food, shelter, clothing, training and work placements. In an appeal in *The Times* in December 1864, the society claimed that through its work hundreds of under sixteen-year-olds had been 'rescued from the streets and dens of London.'[29]

Smaller refuges and societies which worked to rescue child prostitutes and protect others in danger included the Greenwich Mission Home and Deptford Fund Refuge, The Westminster Female Refuge, The National Society for the Protection of Young Girls and the Royal Female Philanthropic Society. However, as with other charitable work, all these efforts were not enough to meet the need and many who sought help, including children, had to be turned away due to lack of funds. Some, as previously discussed, did not want to be rescued because prostitution was often a better option than the alternative ways of making a living. Those prostitutes not controlled by pimps and brothel owners were often content with their lot. They could achieve economic independence, their own room, a better standard of living and control of their lives, albeit at the cost of their respectability.

Mayhew considered that prostitution was more of a social problem than a moral one. He could see that prostitutes were not innately immoral and many were forced into the state because of a lack of suitable alternative work. This was a revelation to his readers. The 'great social evil' remained because the underlying social causes needed to be addressed.

The decline in the number of London street children, which began in the 1860s with the introduction of reformatory and industrial schools, was accelerated, slowly at first, by the passing of the 1870 Education Act. This Act of Gladstone's Liberal government paved the way for a national state education system. It was made necessary by the passing of the 1867 Reform Act, which had extended the vote to working-class householders in the boroughs. It was feared that if the working classes remained uneducated they would not use their vote wisely. As Robert Lowe, an MP and member of the Board of Education, expressed it: 'We must educate our future masters'.

Under the terms of the 1870 Education Act, the government built elementary schools in England and Wales wherever there were no voluntary schools. The new schools were to be run by education boards elected by ratepayers. These 'board' schools, which provided a basic education in the three Rs, charged a weekly fee for all but the very poorest children. The 1870 Education Act, and those which followed, made a considerable impact on the lives of the street children in the later Victorian period and marked the first tentative moves towards a solution to the problem they posed.

THE LATER VICTORIAN PERIOD
1870–1901

CHAPTER 10

The Changing Scene

Holborn Viaduct extends from Holborn Circus to Newgate Street ... The cost of this improvement was considerably over two millions, and the work occupied six and a half years.

Victoria Street is a modern thoroughfare, stretching from Broad Sanctuary to the railway termini known as Victoria station ... The making of Victoria Street did away with a number of slums which gave Westminster a bad reputation, which now it no longer deserves.

It was in 1882 that the Queen opened the Palace (of Justice) which extends from the Strand to Carey Street, and cost £750,000, while nearly a million and a half had to be paid for the site.

Extracts taken from Anon.,
The Queen's London, A Pictorial and Descriptive Record of the Streets, Buildings, Parks and Scenery of the Great Metropolis in the 59th year of the Reign of Her Majesty Queen Victoria, 1896

The modernisation and expansion of the metropolis continued steadily after 1870. In the later Victorian period, London was transformed into a city befitting its role as the capital and administrative centre of a growing empire 'on which the sun never sets'. During this time Britain's empire expanded to cover a quarter of the world's land mass and to contain a quarter of the world's population.

London in 1870 was a very different place to London in 1837. Although there were still many unhealthy and insanitary districts, the vastly improved sewage and drainage systems meant that it could no longer be described as 'a doomed city'. Clean drinking water was now more widely available, with drinking fountains located across the capital. The construction of two more large cemeteries and the introduction of the practice of cremation further improved public health.

Migration into the capital continued unabated, contributing to a population increase of almost half a million every decade during this period. New immigrants included Jews fleeing pogroms in Eastern Europe in the 1880s. The suburbs expanded ever further and further to accommodate this rising population. The metropolis was more vast and more sprawling than ever, and the term 'Greater London' was first used to describe it. The surrounding countryside and outlying villages were swallowed up bit by bit. The suburbs were largely built by speculative builders, mainly on previously undeveloped land. Most of the new homes were villas and terraced houses. Suburbia was essentially a middle-class preserve, although some of the better-off working classes also moved there, especially after the introduction of workmen's trains with lower fares after 1883. Some of the new houses were close enough to the centre of London to make commuting on foot possible. Living in the suburbs became so popular that in 1881 a guidebook for buyers called *The Suburban Homes of London* was published.

The expansion of the suburbs was facilitated by the continued growth of the railways, both above and below ground. Large areas of the metropolis continued to be transformed by the construction of more railway lines, new termini, goods yards, train sheds and 'monster' hotels for rail passengers. Liverpool Street and Blackfriars were among the new stations built in the later period. More bridges, including Hungerford and Wandsworth Bridges, were built to carry new railway lines across the river into central London. The underground was extended and more suburban railway lines were built, enabling the suburbs to spread even further.

By 1870 London's traffic was flowing more easily but more improvements were still needed. In the later period road widening continued and some important roads were constructed, including Northumberland Avenue, Charing Cross Road and Shaftesbury Avenue. Other improvements included the extension of Cannon Street and Piccadilly Circus, the removal of Temple Bar to ease the flow of traffic along Fleet Street and the removal of more road and bridge tolls. The progress of both road and river traffic was improved by the construction of Tower Bridge, an amazing feat of engineering and grand design, built in 1895. New road bridges were built and old ones rebuilt. The remaining muddy river banks and ancient stairways were cleared away with the completion of the Victoria, Albert and Chelsea Embankments. New quays replaced the old wharves and the docks in the East End were demolished and replaced with the Royal Albert, West India, Surrey and Tilbury Docks in the 1880s. These new docks, with roads linking them, were the largest in the world, appropriate for an imperial capital.

Public transport in London continued to improve after 1870. The underground was extended with the opening of four new lines. The omnibus, now improved and more comfortable, remained a much-used form of transport for short distances. In

1. Charles Dickens as a young man.

2. Charles Dickens in later life.

3. Street children.

4. Street children.

Right: 5. Scene in Petticoat Lane.

Below: 6. A Saturday night street market.

7. Stalls in Bishopsgate Street.

8. Street sellers in
Houndsditch, East London.

Right: 9. A street coffee stall.

Below: 10. Covent Garden Market.

11. The Lucifer Match Girl.

12. The Wallflower Girl.

13. The Street-Seller of Grease-Removing
Composition.

14. Street Acrobats Performing.

15. The Hindoo-Tract Seller.

16. The Mudlark.

17. A young mother selling flowers.

18. The One-Legged Road Sweeper of Chancery Lane.

Left: 19. A boy crossing-sweeper at work.

Below: 20. The Newspaper Boys.

Above: 21. The Pool of London, where many mudlarks worked.

Right: 22. Oliver Twist and Fagin.

23. Oliver Twist watching the
Artful Dodger at work.

24. The Bull's Eye.

Right: 25. Newgate Exercise Yard.

Below: 26. Newgate Prison, where many of London's child criminals were incarcerated.

27. Holloway Prison, one of the new prisons built to accommodate the rapidly increasing number of convicted criminals.

28. St George's Street (Ratcliff Highway), East London, a notorious haunt of prostitutes and criminals.

Above: 29. Dudley Street in the Seven Dials slum district.

Right: 30. Slum tenements.

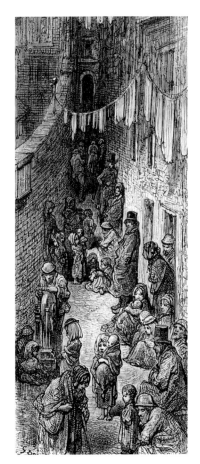

Above: 31. The kitchen of a common lodging house.

Left: 32. The Gin Palace.

33. Homeless people asleep on hayboats on the Thames.

34. Homeless mothers and children.

Left: 35. Destitute people applying for admittance at a refuge.

Below: 36. A Scripture Reader in a Night Shelter.

Above: 37. At the
Hospital Gate.

Right: 38. Afternoon
in the Park. The
parks where
homeless children
slept at night were
frequented by
the better classes
during the day.

39. The Earl of Shaftesbury in 1856.

York Place, Strand.

40. The Off Alley Ragged School.

41. Young ragged school firewood sellers.

42. The training ship *Arethusa* for poor boys belonging to the National Refuge for Destitute Children.

43. Dr Thomas Barnardo.

44. The donkey shed in which Dr Barnardo set up his first ragged school.

45. Jim Jarvis showing Dr Barnardo where some of his friends slept.

46. The corporate seal of the Waifs and Strays Society.

Above: 47a & b. Edward Rudolf, founder of the Waifs and Strays Society.

Right: 48. Children rescued by the Waifs and Strays Society.

49. Street children on a winter's day in north London.

50. Found in the Street.

Right: 51.
Congestion on
London Bridge.

Below: 52. The
Crystal Palace,
built to house the
Great Exhibition
of 1851.

53. Scene at a London underground station.

54. St Pancras Station, opened in 1868.

Above: 55. Blackfriars Bridge, opened in 1869, one of the new bridges built over the Thames to ease traffic congestion in London.

Below: 56. Over London by Rail.

57. Charing Cross Hotel, which opened in 1865.

58. The Imperial Institute in South Kensington, opened in 1893, was built to celebrate Queen Victoria's Golden Jubilee, and to cement the British Empire.

59. The Foreign and India Offices, completed in 1873, was one of the many new public buildings of the later Victorian period.

60. Covent Garden Theatre, built in 1858.

61. The Victoria Embankment, constructed between 1864 and 1870.

62. Regent Street; a late Victorian view of the fashionable shopping street.

63. Victoria Street, built in the 1850s on a site previously occupied by slums.

64. The Royal Courts of Justice, completed in 1883, was built on a site previously occupied by slums.

65. Seven Dials in the later Victorian period, after this slum district had been improved.

66. Tower Bridge, opened in 1886, was a great feat of Victorian engineering.

67. The offices of the London School Board, established in 1870.

68. A cookery class at a London Board School.

69. A carpentry class at a London Board School.

70. Morning Assembly at a London Board School.

the suburbs the horse-drawn tram, first seen in the 1860s, became more popular in the next two decades as the network expanded. For a long time after the arrival of the railway the horse still had an important job to do transporting goods and passengers around the metropolis. Bicycles, a few motor cars and finally motor buses appeared in London during this period.

Visitors and tourists continued to flock to the capital and up-to-date guides, pocket atlases and handbooks were published for their use. Places added to the list of recommended sights included new public buildings in Whitehall, the Royal Albert Hall, the Albert Memorial, the Imperial Institute, the Kensington museums, the recently modernised docks and, later on, Tower Bridge. The re-located Crystal Palace in Sydenham also became a popular place for visitors with a concert hall, a theatre, exhibition galleries, a menagerie and pleasure grounds among its attractions. More amenities were built in later Victorian London for tourists and visitors, including hotels, restaurants, theatres and music halls. Many of these were built in elaborate palatial styles. Parks and open spaces acquired for the public at this time included Battersea Park, Clapham Common and Hampstead Heath. Alexandra Park, with its palace built to rival the Crystal Palace, was opened in 1873 but had to be rebuilt two years later after being destroyed by fire.

London's scenery and skyline changed frequently in the last decades of the century as old buildings were pulled down and new ones appeared. The Law Courts were built between 1874 and 1883. The site of this Gothic-revival style edifice was formerly a notorious slum district north of the Strand. More grand neo-classical buildings were erected in Whitehall, including the Home Office, the Education Office – signifying the government's new role in this area – and the Foreign, Colonial and India Offices required for imperial administration. The Admiralty offices were also extended and the Metropolitan Police Headquarters moved to New Scotland Yard on the embankment. The wholesale markets, so familiar to the child street sellers, had all been extended or rebuilt by the late 1880s. New churches built to serve the ever growing population included Holy Trinity in Sloane Street, the Brompton Oratory and St Mary Abbot's in Kensington. Many new hospitals were also built, including King's College Hospital in Denmark Hill and Brompton Hospital.

The board schools built following the 1870 Education Act were a new architectural feature on the metropolitan landscape at this time. These schools were often large, imposing buildings of several storeys, rising above the surrounding streets as a symbol of the growing importance of education. Mechanics' institutes for the education and self-improvement of the working man, many of whom were recently enfranchised by the 1867 Reform Act, were also built in the later part of the century.

In *Life in the London Streets: or Struggles for Daily Bread*, Richard Rowe described the transformation of London as follows:

London nowadays is being pulled down and built up again on so extensive a scale, and the new buildings are so unlike the old ones they supplant, that many parts of the huge city we see are as identical with those places as we remember them, as the knife that has been rehandled and rebladed, and the gun that has received a new lock, stock and barrel were with the original weapons.[1]

It is difficult to be certain whether crime levels in London went up or down at this time, although the building of Wormwood Scrubs Prison between 1874 and 1891 would appear to suggest the former. A number of factors make it difficult to compare general crime figures between the earlier and later periods. These factors include the addition of new crimes to the statute book and an increase in the number of arrests made as policing improved. The fact that crime always increased during severe winters and at times when wages fell and prices rose also distorted the figures. Violent crime, however, had gone down. The number of those in custody for violent crime in 1891 was only 216 per 100,000 of the population, compared with 378 per 100,000 in 1831.[2] As a result of notorious crimes, such as the Jack the Ripper murders, there was a perception that later Victorian London was a violent and dangerous place. In fact it was, on the whole, a safer place due to the increasing success of the larger and more professional police force. The police were also more accepted by the population than they had been during the 1830s and 1840s. Better street lighting, improved communications, the use of photographs and, at the end of the century, the invention of fingerprinting all helped the police in the fight against crime. However, there were still areas where danger and violence were a daily reality. There was a small decline in the scale of drunkenness but no decline in the other social evil of prostitution.

One grim feature of the metropolitan scene which persisted throughout this period was the slums. Although fewer in number, the slums were more appalling than ever. As more and more of these districts were demolished to make way for improvements, the diminishing number of slum homes became increasingly overcrowded, dilapidated and insanitary. It has been estimated that between 1853 and 1901 the railways alone displaced 76,000 people in London,[3] with no alternative provision made for those rendered homeless until legislation was finally passed in the 1880s. Even after the passing of this Act, many development companies failed to honour their legal responsibilities.

Although the remaining slums were located throughout the metropolis, it was the East End which became most notorious for poverty and deprivation in the later period. Its population increased rapidly by further outward movement from the city and the influx of 140,000 Jewish settlers. People continued to be attracted to the East End and it became a magnet for society's outcasts, which resulted in even greater competition for jobs and housing. The attention of social investigators, reformers, charities, missions and Churches seemed to be focused on the desperate problems of the East End. It was here that the imagined threat to the middle classes posed by 'outcast London' was centred. A greater awareness of class divisions was another feature of London at this time and was exacerbated by the exodus of the better-off classes to the suburbs, leading to an increasingly segregated population.

In the final decades of the nineteenth century, the first efforts were made by charities and individuals to provide purpose-built houses for the working classes. Grim, uniform blocks of flats began to appear on the London scene. In 1888 the London County Council was formed and took over the work of the Metropolitan Board of Works. In time it turned its attention to the urgent task of providing municipal housing for the poor.

Throughout the later Victorian period, the street children remained a visible presence in London. They were like an ugly stain on the landscape, and a source of much shame in the eyes of many people, as modernisation continued and a city worthy to be called the capital of a great empire emerged. The story of these children continued to unfold against this changing background and, with time, solutions to the worrying problems they created began to materialise.

CHAPTER 11

The Later Social Investigative Journalists and Other Writers

This statement is made as the result of a long, patient and sober inquiry, undertaken for the purpose of discovering the actual state of the case and the remedial actions most likely to be effective.

Andrew Mearns
The Bitter Cry of Outcast London, 1884

... the work was undertaken to enlist the sympathies of a class not generally given to the study of 'low life'.

George Sims
Preface to *How the Poor Live*, 1893

My object has been to attempt to show the numerical relation which poverty, misery and depravity bear to regular earnings and comparative comfort, and to describe the general conditions under which each class lives.

Charles Booth
Life and Labour of the Poor in London, 1892

After 1870 a second phase of writing appeared on the subject of the London poor. Despite the revelations of the earlier journalists and all the money and effort expended on behalf of London's poorest citizens, their plight remained desperate and was getting worse due to a still rising population and the effects of slum clearance. The revelations of the later journalists and writers caused such an outcry among the better-off classes that the government was finally forced to take action to help the poor of outcast London, whose numbers included the later street children.

These writers made good use of the language and imagery of exploration, which was very apt, as at this time when missionaries were exploring darkest Africa. As a number of writers pointed out, the poor inhabitants of Africa attracted greater attention and concern than the poor much closer to home. In many articles and books 'outcast London' was portrayed as a dark, dangerous and threatening place. Middle-class readers were taken on a thrilling, vicarious journey into unknown territory they would not normally have ventured into. This *terra incognita* was inhabited by a frightening, savage and unclean race who spoke a different language and whose children were depicted as feral, sub-human creatures. Although this language was used to sensationalise their writing for commercial purposes, the images used by these writers were very appropriate. The poor of London were indeed an alien race to the Victorian middle class, whose members were as likely to journey to darkest Africa as to set foot in the grim courts and alleys of the London slums. As in the earlier period, a plethora of writing, much of it illustrated, appeared on this subject and some has been used as a source for the story of the later street children.

One of the first social investigative works of the later period was *London; A Pilgrimage*, which was published in 1872. The text, written by the journalist Blanchard Jerrold, was illustrated by the French artist Gustave Doré. In his introduction Jerrold described himself and Doré as 'pilgrims, wanderers, gipsy-loiterers'[1] journeying through 'the light and shade'[2] of the Victorian metropolis, which he likened to the giant Titan of classical mythology. 'The light' referred to the grand, attractive places inhabited and frequented by the rich and 'the shade' to the dark places inhabited and frequented by the poor. The latter included the slums, the criminal districts and Newgate prison. The juxtaposition of the descriptions and illustrations of the salubrious parts of London with the ugly and sordid was very effective. This work sold well when it was first published in monthly parts and Doré's illustrations in particular made a profound impression. His haunting pictures of groups of hideous-looking ragged people, including children and babies, with despair and resignation etched on their faces, have illustrated many books on Victorian London. Interestingly, some of his illustrations of individuals such as child flower sellers were not so grotesque and disturbing.

Richard Rowe's book *Life in the London Streets or Struggles for Daily Bread*, published in 1881, is a useful source on the lives of the poor in the later period and included some stories of street children. Rowe, clearly influenced by Henry Mayhew, went onto the streets to interview the poor, whose experiences he reported in their own speech and dialect. He was accompanied by an artist who drew on the spot illustrations of the people interviewed. The intention was, as with other journalists, to remove ignorance of the lives of the poor 'by drawing aside the veil which enshrouds the dregs of the population.'[3]

In 1883 George Sims published an important series of articles on the London poor in the periodical *The Pictorial World.* These articles were the result of his investigation, accompanied by the artist Frederick Barnard, into the living conditions of the underclass. Using the language of exploration, Sims guided his readers through the foul slums with the intention of bringing them 'face to face with that dark side of life which the wearers of rose-coloured spectacles turn away from on principle.'⁴ Sims was particularly worried about the young slum dwellers and drew attention to how slum life led to the 'utter destruction of innocence in the young.'⁵ Sims' articles, which were later published as the book *How the Poor Live,* are an excellent source on the appalling living conditions of some of the later street children.

A pamphlet was published in 1884 by the Revd Andrew Mearns which caused a great outcry in London. *The Bitter Cry of Outcast London; An Inquiry into the Condition of the Abject Poor* drew extensively on Sims' articles of the previous year. Using alarmist language, Mearns focused particularly on the lack of religious beliefs and immoral behaviour, including incest, prevalent among London's slum dwellers. He referred to the conditions in the overcrowded, disease-ridden slums as 'horrors which call to mind what we have heard of the middle passage of the slave ship.'⁶ Mearns summed up the existence of child slum dwellers in the following description:

> From the beginning of their lives they are utterly neglected; their bodies and rags are alive with vermin; they are subjected to the most cruel treatment; many of them have never seen a green field, and do not know what it is to go beyond the streets immediately around them, and they often pass the whole day without a morsel of food.⁷

Mearns claimed that all the work being done among the London poor was not even 'a thousandth part of what needs to be done, a hundredth part of what could be done by the Church of Christ.'⁸ He called for 'some combined and organised effort' from 'churches of all denominations',⁹ a call which was heard loud and clear. This pamphlet was important both for what it revealed about the living conditions and immoral behaviour of the late Victorian poor, and because of its role in putting pressure on the government to take action to help the poor. Its impact on middle-class readers was astonishing.

In 1885 the *Pall Mall Gazette* published the findings of a survey of the working-class districts of London carried out by the Marxist Socialist Democratic Federation. This survey revealed that a quarter of Londoners lived in abject poverty. Charles Booth, a businessman with a concern for the poor, did not believe this figure and set out to discover for himself the true extent of poverty in the capital. He systematically investigated London, neighbourhood by neighbourhood and trade by trade. Londoners were divided into eight categories according to their earnings and occupations, which enabled Booth to draw up a colour-coded map of poverty. His scientific study, backed up by statistics, shockingly showed that in fact 30 per cent of Londoners lived a hand-to-mouth existence of chronic want. The study was published in seventeen volumes as *Life and Labour of the People in London,* the first volume of which appeared in 1892. Booth's general study of poverty, supported by particular examples, added to the demands for action to deal with the problem of 'outcast London' and is another valuable historical source.

In the first part of his book *In Darkest England and the Way Out*, published in 1890, William Booth described the dreadful lives of London's 'submerged tenth'. This picture was drawn from his own and his officers' first-hand knowledge of life in the East End slums. Booth likened England to darkest Africa:

> As there is a darkest Africa is there not also a darkest England ... May we not find a parallel at our own doors and discover within a stone's throw of our cathedrals and palaces similar horrors to those which Stanley has found existing in the great Equatorial forest ... As in Africa, it is all trees, trees, trees, with no other world conceivable; so is it here – it is all vice and poverty and crime.[10]

Booth considered the slums of London to be as 'poisonous' as African swamps and pointed out that children were dying in them. He summed up these children in the following words:

> They are in reality starved and poisoned, and all that can be said is that, in many cases, it is better for them that they were taken away from the trouble to come.[11]

This picture added to the mounting evidence of the problem of 'outcast London'. In the second part of his book Booth set out his ultimately unrealised plans to rescue the 'submerged tenth' by founding a self-supporting community.

Other journalists and writers whose work has been drawn on to put together the story of the later street children are Thomas Wright, author of *The Great Army of the London Poor* (1882) and *The Pinch of Poverty* (1892), the Revd D. Rice-Jones, author of *In the Slums* (1884), and the author of *Walks in and Around London* (1895), who wrote under the name of 'Uncle Jonathan'.

CHAPTER 12

Surviving on the Streets

I've been walking the streets almost day and night these two weeks and can't get work. I've got the strength, though I shan't have it long at this rate. I only want a job. This is the third night running that I've walked the streets all night; the only money I get is by minding blacking-boys' boxes while they go into Lockhart's for their dinner. I got a penny yesterday at it, and twopence for carrying a parcel, and today I've had a penny. Bought a ha'porth of bread and a ha'penny mug of tea.

A homeless London street boy interviewed by a Salvation Army Officer.
General William Booth
Darkest England and The Way Out, 1890

Flowers I works mostly when they're in. Yes, flowers is nice to look at an' to smell, but that's for them as buys, not them as sells, to think about. I'd work anythink as I could git money to buy grub an' shoes an' clo'es, an' 'ud leave me stock-money to go on with.

Sometimes I haven't got a shoe to my foot. I don't care much in summer, but it's orful cold in winter, my toes gits swollen up like taturs wi' the chilblains. Any old think I'll buy second-hand to kiver me, but there's precious little warmth in some on 'em. It's grub, I thinks, as keeps you warmest, if you can git enough on it, that, an' a drop o' hot cawfee or summat like that, now an' agin, to drink.

The Story of the Flower Girl,
Richard Rowe
Life in London: or Struggles For Daily Bread, 1881

The number of street children in London began to decline after 1870 but they remained such an obvious presence that some contemporaries did not notice this. A few even thought that the number of street children had increased. Thomas Wright, who wrote under the pseudonym of 'The Riverside Visitor', wrote in 1882 that:

Many individual children have been rescued; but the class increases rather than diminishes, is to be numbered by hundreds of thousands.[1]

Both the feral and better type of street children continued to be lumped together and described in the same derogatory language used in the earlier period. They were still referred to as 'street arabs', 'guttersnipes', and 'hottentots' who roamed, swarmed and prowled like wild animals and lived in 'lairs' and 'haunts'. Writers and commentators who were sympathetic to the plight of the street children still unthinkingly failed to distinguish between the two types. The continued use of negative language revealed the unease and fear which these children still provoked; they remained a subject of much debate and concern.

Universal state education, which led to the gradual decrease in the number of children on the London streets, was at first provided only for children between the ages of five and ten. Older children were, consequently, still seen working on the streets or hanging around them. Attendance in London schools became compulsory in 1880, by which time enough schools had been built to provide a place for every child, but it was difficult to enforce for some time.

Many poor parents kept their children, especially girls, at home to help with domestic chores or to mind younger siblings. The 'little mothers' were, therefore, still much in evidence on slum streets. Poor parents had also been used to relying on the paid work of their children outside the home and often defied the school authorities by keeping them away to earn money. It took a long time for many parents to accept the importance of school and that it had to come before work during school hours and terms, whatever their home circumstances. Those parents who were not exempt from paying the school pence and could not spare the money often kept their children at home for this reason. To begin with the education authorities and magistrates were lenient about attendance, which meant that it was some time before the introduction of compulsory education for the poor began to make a noticeable difference to the number of London street children. Out of school hours and during holidays, the streets were as full of children as they had always been.

The later street children followed the same occupations as those of the earlier period; they sold goods, scavenged, entertained and performed, ran errands, provided services, begged, committed crime and worked as prostitutes. Their life stories remained popular subjects for journalists and writers, and were a source of continued fascination and concern for their middle-class readers.

Richard Rowe met a number of children selling on the streets of later Victorian London and recorded their stories in *Episodes in an Obscure Life* (1871) and *Life in the London Streets; or Struggles for Daily Bread* (1881). One child he interviewed was an illiterate seller of oranges and nuts called Mike, an orphan who worked with his younger sister Jenny. These children were the survivors of four siblings, one of whom had died from a fever caught while sleeping on the streets. Rowe described Mike as:

a squalidly dressed, stunted touzled-headed urchin, with not much more prominence of nose than that on the monkey-faces at the end of the shaggy-shelled cocoa-nuts round about; with a mere slit of a mouth, but with white teeth in it, and a merry smile upon it, which, ugly though he was, made a sunshine in that shady place.[2]

On the death of their father, Mike's mother had been forced to leave her young children locked up all day while she worked as a street seller to support them. Mike and Jenny became sellers themselves and survived by this means following their mother's death. Kind neighbours had helped them for a while to keep them out of the workhouse. When Rowe met Mike, the children were fending for themselves and were engaged in a constant battle against hunger and cold. Sometimes they could not even afford the shelter of a common lodging house. Mike stated that:

It's as much as me and Jenny can do often to get food, and sometimes we can't do that, and have to sleep anywhere we can, like the sparrows, but not half as snug.[3]

Although it was some years since the passing of the 1870 Education Act, these children had not received any education at all and Mike, who was used to the freedom of the streets, declared that 'I should choke if I was cooped up in a school.'[4] The children were very protective of each other and intended to stay together. As Mike expressed it:

... me and Jenny mean to work together always. We're safe not to cheat each other, and one don't grudge the other full share of anything that's going, and that's more than you can say of a good many of them that work together.[5]

Mike was one of the better class of street children who strove in a dignified manner to make an honest living. His courage, resilience, cheerfulness, lack of self pity and acceptance of his lot were reminiscent of some of the children interviewed by Mayhew in the 1840s.

Children continued to earn money by scavenging for anything of value on the streets, in the sewers and on the banks of the Thames. In his book *In the Slums*, published in 1884, the Revd D. Rice-Jones recorded an encounter with a group of child mudlarks 'swarming'[6] near Vauxhall Bridge one cold winter morning. If the day in question was a school day, those children under ten must have been playing truant, an illustration of the flouting of the requirement for school attendance. Rice-Jones counted between fifty and one hundred 'boys and girls of all ages from six or seven up to fourteen or fifteen, some of them knee-deep in the water, and others knee-deep in the mud.'[7] Like the children seen by Mayhew, these waifs were dressed in tattered rags and their faces were etched with hunger and misery. Their observer noted 'how earnestly' and 'patiently' the boys searched for pieces of coal and wood and 'how bravely they all trudged in the water and endured the rain, wind and cold.'[8] Their courage and dignity in the face of extreme adversity moved him so much that he described it as 'one of the most touching, if not one of the most noble sights'[9] he had ever witnessed.

Child performers were still much in evidence on the streets of London after 1870. Dr Barnardo met one agile young performer after watching him from the top of an omnibus in the East End. He left the following description of the encounter in his memoirs:

> ... we could not outpace the ragged youngster, who managed not only to keep well abreast of our vehicle, but to secure time enough to enable him every now and then to go down on his hands, and to spin with wild energy several complete and neatly executed 'catherines'. Of course halfpence were thrown to him, and these I observed that he secreted, as such boys generally do, in his mouth.[10]

The boy followed Barnardo when he got off the bus and got into conversation with him. He was the son of a 'drunken and immoral creature who cared little or nothing for her unfortunate son',[11] with the result that the boy had to fend for himself on the streets all day. He crept home at night time to shelter in the slum room his mother occupied. Frank, as the boy was called, jumped at the opportunity of entering Barnardo's home in Stepney when this was suggested. As he was not an orphan his mother's consent had to be obtained first but this proved to be no obstacle and the boy was able to begin a new life. Dr Barnardo noticed an instant change in Frank.

> It was quite marvellous to notice, after he was washed and cleaned, what an attractive and interesting boy he really appeared, while it was soon evident that he possessed more than an average share of shrewdness and native wit.[12]

Under the care of the staff in the Stepney Home for Boys Frank soon made up for the years of neglect and abuse he had endured, and flourished. His story, at least, had a happy ending.

Among the children who survived in the later period by providing services on the streets of London were a brother and sister whose story was told by Richard Rowe in *Episodes in an Obscure Life,* published in 1871. Fred and Emily worked all week on a city crossing and outside an East End church every Sunday. These polite and well behaved children, who were the orphaned offspring of a doctor described as 'a bad sort', had been turned out onto the streets when their mother died. Their middle-class background was evident in their refined features and tidy, though ragged, appearance. Fred and Emily also differed from other street children in that, having swept the crossing for the congregation on the way to church, they then crept into the back pews themselves to listen to the service.

One Sunday Rowe was surprised to see an elderly man in the children's place at the crossing and learned from him that Fred was ill and his sister was looking after him. The man shared the children's 'lodgings' in a converted stable under a railway arch. Rowe was deeply shocked at the plight of these children when he was taken to see them. With the help of a clergyman, Rowe managed to find a place for them in an orphanage where, in the words of the old man who had lived with them, 'you are a-goin' to be brought up respectable.'[13]

Thomas Wright, 'The Riverside Visitor', met several children in the early 1880s who survived by running errands for people on the streets. One such child was a ten-year-old boy called 'Kiddy' Miller who shared a slum room with his friend and the friend's mother. Wright recorded a conversation with this 'bare-footed, ragged, dirty and hungry-looking boy' who was both a 'gutter-child' and a 'nobody's child'.[14] Having been deserted by his cruel widowed mother, 'Kiddy' was forced to survive 'on his own hook'. He made money or 'browns' by carrying parcels and pushing barrows. If he could save enough money to buy stock, 'Kiddy' also did a spot of street selling. When he could find no work this cheerful lad survived by stealing food and eating the sweepings of rotten fruit and vegetables from greengrocers' shops. He found 'the gripes' he sometimes got from bad food to be preferable to 'the gnawin' when yer hasn't had nothin'" and at least he enjoyed the benefit of the 'blow-out' first.[15]

The only education this boy had received was at a ragged school which he briefly attended, mainly for the food on offer. Thomas Wright summed up 'Kiddy's' future prospects as 'either hard, precarious, ill-paid labour or criminality – with the chances inclining more to the latter than the former.'[16] With the premature wisdom of the street child, 'Kiddy' was well aware of this himself. His story has similarities with many related by Mayhew in the earlier period.

In the later period, fewer street children survived by crime than previously. This was revealed in a report of 1894 by Henry Rogers, Assistant Inspector of Reformatories and Industrial Schools. He stated that:

> Boys are not so criminal or so difficult to deal with as they used to be. We do not have the same education in crime that we had ... You can see from the experience of everyday life that the newspapers do not report cases of pickpockets now; a few years ago there was nothing heard of in the public courts but 'pocket dipping' as they called it.[17]

The new reformatory and industrial schools, with their emphasis on discipline, hard work and moral and industrial training, had finally helped to break the cycle of juvenile crime and contributed to a marked decrease in the juvenile crime rate in the later period. The work of social reformers and reform societies contributed to this decline too. A more humane and understanding attitude towards child criminals also helped, as well as education for the poor, improving standards of living and an accompanying gradual improvement in social conditions.

However, the vagrant life remained attractive to some youths, as illustrated by the following story told by Richard Rowe in *Life in the London Streets*. It is the story of a ragged, dirty lad nicknamed 'the Limb' who was pursued by Rowe's friend after he picked his pocket. The boy had never known his father and his mother was a drunken thief who, in the words of her neighbour, 'don't care nought about him, 'cept when he brings her money for the things he's prigged or what he's begged.'[18] The boy survived on food given by neighbours, when they could spare it, and the profits of begging and stealing. Rowe's friend offered 'The Limb' a home in his housekeeper's quarters with 'plenty to eat by a good fire in the kitchen, and a snug little room and nice warm bed down there'[19] as well as the chance to go to school. At first the boy did well and seemed happy but soon 'he felt painfully the restraint of the civilizing process to which he was being subjected.'[20] Before long he ran away because 'he could hear the rumbling of the streets and longed for Arab liberty once more.'[21] The call of the streets proved too strong for 'The Limb' and he remained one of the declining number of young criminals and ruffians on the London streets at this time.

Prostitution remained a means of earning money for young girls, as juvenile prostitutes were as much in evidence in the metropolis after 1870 as before. The demand for young girls was as high as ever and they continued to be forced onto the streets by their poor families or went of their own accord. Despite pressure from evangelical Christians, the government's attitude towards prostitution continued to be one of non-intervention and little could, therefore, be done to suppress it.

In the 1880s, however, public opinion on the issue began to change when William Stead, the editor of the *Pall Mall Gazette*, embarked on a campaign against child prostitution. He sought to prove the existence of trafficking in young girls for English and European brothels by 'buying' the thirteen-year-old daughter of a poor London chimney sweep. He then wrote a series of articles under the title of 'The Maiden Tribute of Modern Babylon' in his magazine to expose this vile trade. Although the girl was immediately handed over to the Salvation Army to be looked after, Stead was imprisoned for the offence of child abduction. He had succeeded in his object, however, as his article caused a huge sensation and outcry which led to the passing of the Criminal Law Amendment Act in 1885. This Act raised the age of consent to sixteen years, punished those who permitted under-age sex on their premises and made it a criminal offence to abduct a girl under the age of eighteen for sexual purposes. The effects of the new Act were soon evident and children, at last, received some protection against being forced into prostitution against their will.

The more understanding attitude towards child criminals and the protection for children provided by the Criminal Law Amendment Act were part of a change of feelings about poor children which emerged after 1870. There was a growing concern for them and a new awareness of their needs. Soon, the children at the bottom of the social pyramid would be protected and properly looked after by adults, rather than being expected to grow up long before their time.

CHAPTER 13

Helping the Later Street Children

Never in the history of the Church or the world has such an organised attempt been made to rescue the destitute from starvation, the suffering from peril, and the downtrodden and cruelly ill-used little ones from their oppressors and tormentors. Never before have the hands of loving sympathy been held out so widely or so effectively to the orphaned and the helpless. Never before has any one man borne so large a share of responsibility in such a cause, and never before were there so many children saved in a single year and placed with their faces heavenward as our records for 1892 exhibit.

Dr Barnardo, 1892

Dr Stephenson's Children's Home, at Victoria Park, is one amongst many others engaged in giving a fresh start in life to many a destitute and friendless boy or girl ... In these Homes everything that can be done is done to enable the children to overcome their bad habits, and to fit them for some useful occupation when they leave the Home. Industry and intelligence, order and cleanliness, cheerfulness and activity, are encouraged; religion is inculcated; and the whole discipline through which the children pass cultivates and improves them so much, that it is difficult to recognise in these sturdy, active, intelligent boys and girls leaving the Home, the pale-faced, poor, neglected ones who entered it some years before.

'Uncle Jonathan'
Walks In and Around London, 1895.

The street children of the later period had one important advantage over their earlier counterparts; they did not have to struggle on alone because there was much more help available to them. Philanthropists and charities already involved in rescuing London's homeless and destitute children continued and increased their efforts, while others joined in the rescue work. In 1869 the Charity Organisation Society was set up to oversee the work of London charities and make sure charitable effort was directed at the 'deserving poor'.

Dr Barnardo's business talent, strong leadership and organisational skills led to a great expansion of his work after 1870. With the involvement of many wealthy and influential people, donations flowed in to aid his cause. One way in which funds were raised was by selling 'before and after' pictures of the children rescued. Many of the buildings which housed the children were given outright or to use rent free. Among the distinguished people who became involved in Dr Barnardo's work was Earl Cairns, the Lord Chancellor, who was the first president of the charity, and Princess Mary of Teck, who became a patron.

As well as orphans and children of cruel and neglectful parents, Dr Barnardo took in children no-one else wanted, including prostitutes and criminals. He continued to go out at night, often accompanied by boys from his homes, seeking children who were sleeping rough and those in common lodging houses. He became known as the 'young man with the lantern'. In the 1870s Dr Barnardo opened more homes in London and adopted the policy of never turning away a destitute child following the death on the streets of a boy for whom he had been unable to find room. An all-night shelter was opened at 10 Stepney Causeway, to rescue children at all hours of the day and night, as well as an infirmary for sick children. Dr Barnardo set up a City Messengers Brigade in 1870 to provide further job opportunities for boys, and continued his work of educating poor children by opening more ragged schools. These schools provided food as well as education for the needy slum children who attended.

In 1874 Dr Barnardo began to accept girls, and in 1876 he opened a village home in Barkingside in Essex where girls could be brought up in cottages under the care of a housemother, which was thought to be a more suitable environment for them than a large orphanage. In 1877 a Deaconess Home was founded at Bow to train women to work in Barnardo homes, and to minister to the poor in general. By the end of the decade this work of rescuing children was extended beyond the capital, and homes for sick and disabled children were established.

New departures in the 1880s included the establishment of homes for babies and very young children, a children's hospital in East London, training homes for older girls, two centres from whence boys were put out to sea and a free lodging house in Spitalfields providing temporary shelter. The most important development of this decade, however, was the commencement of an emigration scheme under which children were sent out to Canada to start a new life. Jim Jarvis, the boy who originally alerted Dr Barnardo to the plight of London's destitute children, was the first emigrant. Initially the doctor had reservations about this idea, but eventually came to accept the merits of 'well planned and wisely conducted child emigration.'[1] One reason for his change of mind was that, in the words of his first biographers, an ever-open door required an 'ever-open exit'.[2] Dr Barnardo needed to off-load some of his charges in order to make room for more needy children. A home and distribution centre was opened in Ontario, from where emigrants were placed in new homes to begin work as farm labourers or domestic servants. A support system was put in place to help these young emigrants. The scheme not only benefited the children by offering them opportunities not available in England but was also of benefit to Canada which, as a growing colony, was in great need of young workers. Some of the children sent out to Canada made a success of their new lives but for others, unfortunately, it was not a happy experience. There were cases of children having to be removed from homes where they were treated badly.

The emigration scheme enabled Dr Barnardo to rescue more of London's street children in the 1890s as well as further extending his work across the country. Another development was the 'boarding out' of children, a practice used in England since the 1870s by Boards of Guardians with pauper children in their care. The Barnardo children were placed in the countryside, away from the unhealthy, overpopulated metropolis. Homes were found with respectable, industrious working-class families. Careful vetting of foster parents and their homes was carried out and a proper contract drawn up to keep boarded out children safe and properly provided for. Visiting doctors watched over and supported them. As with emigration, this arrangement benefited both the children concerned and the families who took them in, as the latter received a welcome addition to their income. A further advantage was that children were placed in depopulated country areas in need of reinvigoration.

Alongside rescuing London's destitute children, Dr Barnardo continued his mission work among the poor in general. This work included the opening of two coffee palaces in the East End to encourage teetotalism, as he knew that many children were abused and neglected because of their parents' addiction to alcohol. Dr Barnardo encountered a number of setbacks and a considerable amount of criticism during the many years he worked amongst the poorest inhabitants of Victorian London. He recorded in his memoirs that he often worked 'in the very teeth of the bitterest prejudice and opposition'[3] but he undoubtedly deserved the claim of his first biographers that he was 'the champion' of voluntary efforts to help England's destitute and homeless children. In 1889, Dr Barnardo summed up his work in the following words:

> For nearly a quarter of a century ... I and my colleagues have been actively at work, by day and night, engaged in rescuing from the slums of London, from the vilest haunts of the lapsed masses, from houses of ill-fame, from positions generally of suffering, danger and moral contamination, children and young people of both sexes, of almost any age, without respect to creed, nationality or physical condition, the only passport of eligibility being destitution.[4]

According to Mrs Barnardo and James Marchant in *Memoirs of the Late Dr Barnardo*, he 'helped during his lifetime, more or less permanently, a quarter of a million children, nearly sixty thousand of whom he maintained, educated and started in life under his own roof'.[5] This number included countless London street children.

The rescue work started by Charles Spurgeon and Thomas Stephenson also expanded in the later Victorian period. Financial and other aid poured in to enable Spurgeon's boys' home at Stockwell to flourish and for a girls' wing to be opened in 1879. Children of all denominations were admitted, as need was the only criterion for entry. Spurgeon was much loved by the children he rescued and he maintained a personal involvement and interest in their lives.

Stephenson's work went from strength to strength after 1870. From the outset he placed children in small houses with house-parents because he wanted them to experience a loving family life, which was not possible in a large institution. In 1871 Stephenson's homes were accepted as part of the responsibility of the Methodist Church, and he eventually gave up his ministry to concentrate on his work with the children. Like Dr Barnardo, Stephenson went out at night seeking 'ownerless children' and created a national network of homes in which children were trained for the future as well as looked after. He also used trained sisters to help run his homes and minister to the poor, and he sent children abroad to start a new life. Stephenson succeeded in his objective of training children through love. One of the boys he rescued described him as a friend and explained that 'a friend is a bloke wot knows all about yer – and – still loves yer and he's my friend'.[6]

In 1882 the Church of England became involved in the work of rescuing London's destitute and homeless children. Two brothers, Edward and Robert de Montjoie Rudolf, who worked as Sunday school teachers in South London, became worried when two of their regular pupils suddenly stopped attending. The boys were found begging on the streets in a very neglected condition. On learning that the boys' father had recently died, leaving their mother to support and bring up seven young children unaided, the Rudolfs tried but failed to get them into an orphanage which did not require payment. This alerted them to the fact that, despite the efforts of Dr Barnardo and others engaged in rescuing children, there was a great need for more homes. The Rudolf brothers, therefore, established the Church of England Central Society for Providing Homes for Waifs and Strays, and opened its first home in Dulwich in 1882. The society, which grew rapidly, aimed for its children to be fostered or adopted and to become part of the communities in which they lived. The Archbishop of Canterbury was the first president of the society and other influential people, such as the Lord Mayor of London, became involved in its work. Like other such organisations, the society's net spread across the country and a home was opened for emigrants in Canada. Receipts from donations, legacies and fundraising increased every year. In the last year of Victoria's reign the society took its largest ever receipts, and the number of children in its care had risen to 2,826.[7]

The great outpouring of compassion for the poor, needy and distressed flowed on. The later street children, including criminals and prostitutes, benefited from the continued assistance of many charities and organisations such as the city missions and the Salvation Army. In 1882 the Church Army was founded and added hundreds of trained evangelists and mission nurses to those already engaged in helping the metropolitan poor. The Church Army built labour, rescue and lodging homes as well as homes for children, discharged prisoners and alcoholics. It also took over the work of the Houseless Poor Society.

The London poor, including the street children, continued to help each other as well. The author of *Walks In and Around London,* published in 1895, who wrote under the pseudonym of 'Uncle Jonathan', noted how 'some of these poor, dirty children helped those who are poorer still'.[8] One of the stories he related was that of a group of young street workers who scraped together eighteen pence to pay for food and lodgings for another boy who was even worse off than they were.

In the later Victorian period a more understanding and sympathetic attitude towards the poor emerged. They began to be perceived more as victims of circumstances beyond their control than as authors of their own misfortune. The social investigative journalists and writers of both the early and late periods had helped to bring about this kinder attitude. This new perception of poverty led to a more understanding view of the street children.

The work of the organisations involved in saving destitute children played a significant part in these changing perceptions. A very important aspect of the work of Dr Barnardo and others involved in helping needy children was that they publicised their plight, made helping them acceptable and set an example in the way they should be treated. They showed what could be achieved if unwanted children were given the love, care and attention of which the majority of them had been deprived and which most better-off children took for granted. They demonstrated that with education, training, kindness, attention and proper care even the worst kind of street child could make something of his life. The child rescue organisations also highlighted the deficiencies of the state in dealing with the problem. As Mrs Barnardo and James Marchant wrote in *Memoirs Of The Late Dr Barnardo*:

> In showing what voluntary effort, of which he was the champion, can accomplish, he has aroused State officials, whilst emphasising their failures and limitations, to make more use of their peculiar powers as guardians and treasurers of the people's blood and money.[9]

In time, it came to be accepted that poor children, like their better-off counterparts, also deserved a special period in their lives when they were protected and sheltered before adult responsibilities descended upon them. Although many poor children were still required to make a financial contribution to their family income and do household chores some, at least, of their responsibilities were lifted. As will be seen later, parents were made to face up to their responsibilities, and adults from outside the family became involved in the lives of poor children, with the result that they were allowed to be children for longer.

The changing attitude towards poor and vulnerable children gave rise to an awareness of their needs and a concern for their welfare. This led to the founding of anti-cruelty societies. In 1884 the London Society for the Prevention of Cruelty to Children was founded by the Revd Benjamin Waugh, who had seen for himself the degradation and cruelty experienced by children in Greenwich, where he lived. The priority of the society was to draw attention to the plight of suffering children. By 1889 there were thirty-two branches of the society in England, Wales and Scotland, which amalgamated to become the National Society for the Prevention of Cruelty to Children,[10] with Queen Victoria as its patron. The society employed inspectors to investigate cases of abuse and neglect.

In the same year the Prevention of Cruelty to, and Protection of Children Act, also known as the Children's Charter, was passed. This was a very important milestone because, for the first time, children were given their own rights as individuals. It meant that the state could henceforth intervene in the relationship between parents or guardians and children in order to protect the latter.[11] Until the introduction of this Act, children had been the property of their parents or guardians to treat, or mistreat, as they saw fit. Adults could now be arrested for mistreating children and homes could be entered to protect children suspected of being at risk. Those convicted of cruelty or other abuse could be fined, imprisoned and lose custody of their children.

This Act directly affected the street children because it included restrictions on child employment and outlawed child begging. It prohibited boys aged ten to fourteen years and girls aged ten to sixteen years from being employed as paid performers or singers. It also prohibited them from selling goods on the streets or in licensed premises, with the exception of licensed public amusement venues, between 10 p.m. and 5 a.m. Younger children were banned completely from such work and punishments were laid down for adults who caused children to break this law.[12] Acts passed in 1894 and 1903 put further resrictions on the employment of children and provided safeguards to protect them. Although the control of child employment was undoubtedly for the better, the new restrictions must have made life more difficult for some street children in the short term.

The kinder attitude towards poor children, including those on the streets, was reflected in new terminology used to describe them. Although they were still called 'street arabs' and 'gutter children', they were also now referred to as 'waifs', most notably in the name chosen for their rescue society by the Rudolf brothers. This new name, with its suggestion of frailty, helplessness and victimhood, was much more fitting.

Despite the increased help for London's street children and the resulting decline in their numbers, they remained a feature of the late Victorian metropolis. As already noted, some children chose to remain on the streets because they enjoyed the freedom and independence this lifestyle allowed. Not all children were happy to submit to the disciplined and ordered life offered by Dr Barnardo and other rescuers. Some children never acquired the work ethic necessary to lift themselves out of the underclass and continued to live the disordered and unpredictable life of a vagrant.

CHAPTER 14

Homes of the Later Street Children

As we entered the court children were swarming in all parts of it. Many of them were without shoes or stockings, and all were wretchedly ill-clad and dirty; and while some few among them were robust, the majority had the sickly appearance that comes of habitual hard living, foul dwellings, and uncleanly habits. They were of all ages, from fourteen or fifteen years down to infants of scarcely as many months, who were to be seen crawling unheeded in the gutter. Still younger babies were being carried about much as though they were bundles of rags, by girls, some of whom were little more than infants themselves. The older ones, more particularly the boys, already acquiring loafing habits, were standing about in groups. The younger ones were running about, wildly yelling and shouting; and amid the general noise could be heard language of which it is sufficient to say that it was doubly horrible coming from such young lips. It was not a pretty picture ...

Thomas Wright
The Great Army of London Poor, 1882

Some seven years ago a great outcry was made concerning the Housing of the Poor. Much was said, and rightly said – it could not be said too strongly – concerning the disease-breeding, manhood-destroying character of many of the tenements in which the poor herd in our large cities. But there is a depth below that of the dweller in the slums. It is that of the dweller in the street, who has not even a lair in the slums which he can call his own.

William Booth
In Darkest England and The Way Out, 1890

The street children of the later period slept rough, in lodging houses, in refuges, and lived in slum homes, as their earlier counterparts had done. Although there was more temporary accommodation available for the homeless by the later decades of the century, there were nowhere near enough places for all those in need. Consequently, many of London's homeless, including children, were still compelled to find shelter wherever they could. Salvation Army officers came into contact with London's rough sleepers every night as they patrolled the streets. In his book *In Darkest England And The Way Out*, William Booth noted that popular locations for 'al fresco lodgings in London' included the Thames Embankment and the seats outside Spitalfields church as well as 'little nooks and corners of resort in many sheltered yards, vans etc. all over London'.[1]

Booth recorded the findings of a census taken by a Salvation Army officer one late summer night in the 1880s. A total of 368 people were counted sleeping in the open 'along the line of the Thames from Blackfriars to Westminster', including Covent Garden Market, the recesses of the bridges and along the embankment itself.[2] This census was taken during a period of 'good trade' when more people were in work; the number would have been far higher during bad economic times.

In *Life in the London Streets* Richard Rowe told the sad tale of a homeless girl he found asleep under a street coffee stall. Rowe was shocked to find that what he thought was 'a bundle of mildewed rags' was in fact a girl 'curled up very much like a cat'.[3] The stall holder had given the cold, hungry and exhausted girl some food and a temporary shelter from the cold. Rowe's description of the girl is truly harrowing.

The two or three homeless people who were outside worshippers of the stall's fires were tattered and torn, but their dress was whole and clean in comparison with this poor girl's. I can only liken it, so far as colour and cleanliness are concerned, to the heaps of mud we see scraped up by the roadside: it was as full of holes as a net, but many of its meshes were loose strips of raveled stuff. One foot, shod with dirt as with a sandal-sole, peeped from beneath her dress, and most likely the other had not shoe or stocking either. She had on some kind of little shawl, or rather neckerchief, originally, perhaps, like those worn by milk-women, in which she hunched up her shoulders and folded her hands; but she did not seem to have any under-clothing – at least what looked like dirty flesh showed here and there as faintly lighter streaks and blotches through the gashes in her gown. Perhaps, however, the most pitiable part of her attire was her bonnet. It had been of the tawdry 'fine' kind, and the wire stalks and a few of the flabby, washed-out, and then dirt-engrained calico petals of its artificial flowers were entangled in her tousled hair. Whether her face had ever been pretty I cannot say, it was so disguised in dirt and disfigured by disease. I could not have guessed her age within four or five years, but the stall-keeper declared that she could not be sixteen.[4]

Rowe described this poor girl's life as 'typical of the lot of scores – perhaps I should be nearer the truth if I said hundreds – of young girls in London.'[5] He guessed that she was either an orphan, or had been sent out by her parents to beg or steal, or had fled from a harsh mistress. Rowe thought she may have once lived in a lodging house 'where she was ruined',[6] or may even have spent some time in prison. The suffering she must have endured is impossible to imagine. Rowe summed up his emotions about her with these words:

> It was hard to refrain from wishing that she might never wake again, but cease to live, as she lay on the earth that had been so cruel a step-mother to her, with a heart softened by the first act of kindness she had received, no doubt, for many a day.[7]

The makeshift home of the twin crossing sweepers, whose story was told in a previous chapter, was typical of the 'little nooks and corners' referred to by William Booth. Richard Rowe left the following description of their shelter, which was shaken unnervingly whenever a train rumbled along the railway line overhead:

> A little mouldy hay and straw had been left in the loft by the former tenant and two or three tattered sacks. It is no exaggeration to say that these were its chief furniture. The articles which the incoming tenants had brought in with them, or subsequently acquired, might all have been put into a not very large carpet-bag.[8]

The little crossing sweepers were luckier than the girl seen under the coffee stall because at least they had a shelter of sorts and money to buy food. Nevertheless, young Fred's admission to a fever hospital was no doubt a result of his dreadful living conditions. Richard Rowe's intervention probably saved his life.

The number of common lodging houses had fallen considerably by the later period but many of those remaining were in a poor condition. In 1875 there were 1,241 lodging houses in London but by 1894 there were only 654 and by 1899 only 542.[9] Control of lodging houses had been transferred by this time from the police to the new London County Council. In the 1880s and 1890s there were many clean, respectable and properly run alternative forms of temporary accommodation for the homeless, including large hostels run by the Salvation and Church Armies and the London Congregational Union. Dr Barnardo's temporary shelter in Spitalfields provided accommodation for children seeking a respite from the streets. There was also the option of refuges such as the Field Lane Refuge, which remained in operation.

As in the earlier period, the only other alternative to the streets themselves was the workhouse casual ward. The accommodation in casual wards changed from around 1870 to small cells, like prison cells, instead of large dormitories. Under the new system each small sleeping cell had a working cell attached where the work tasks such as stone breaking or oakum picking were carried out. Men and older boys were housed in one part of the building and women, girls and younger children in another. In return for food and shelter men and boys were given hard physical work to do, while women and girls were given lighter work or domestic tasks. As before, completing the work tasks prevented the 'casuals' from earning money while they were detained, thus perpetuating the poverty they were designed to alleviate. Apart from the introduction of the cellular system, the casual ward remained much the same, as illustrated by the following description of William Booth's:

> There you are taken in, and provided for on the principle of making it as disagreeable as possible for yourself, in order to deter you from again accepting the hospitality of the rates ...[10]

Following the passing of the Casual Poor Act of 1882, people who used the casual wards had to be detained for two nights and work a whole day in between if they were unable to pay for their accommodation. It was forbidden for anyone to return to the same ward within thirty days; those who did were punished by being made to stay for four nights and working for the intervening days. Although London's casual wards continued to offer an occasional respite to the street children, many were put off by the deliberate policy of deterrence. William Booth noticed that most of the homeless preferred to sleep in the open air, despite the vagaries of the English weather, rather than suffer the experience of the casual ward.

Incredibly, the slum homes in which some of the later street children lived were even worse than those of the earlier period. Further modernisation, without alternative provision for the displaced poor, resulted in horrendous overcrowding in the remaining slum housing which, not surprisingly, deteriorated still further. London's abject poor continued to be exploited by ruthless, rack-renting landlords who failed to comply with recent health regulations.

Although slum housing still existed across London, it was the East End which became synonymous with the worst deprivation and suffering in the last decades of the century. The continued movement of population to this area from the City as well as its continued attraction to those in search of casual work and work in the sweated trades resulted in enormous competition for jobs and housing. Further pressure was exerted by the influx of a large number of Jewish people in the 1880s, fleeing persecution in Eastern Europe. Matters were made even worse by the clearance of slum housing to make way for more redevelopment of the docks and connecting roads. During this period the abandonment of the East End by better-off workers who could afford to move out to the suburbs resulted in it becoming a ghetto for the very poorest residents. It was here that the supposed threat posed by 'outcast London' was believed to exist. This belief was strengthened when distress caused by seasonal unemployment and severe weather during the winters of 1879 and 1881 led to bread riots.

It was in the 1880s that the most shocking depictions of 'outcast London' appeared. The social investigators, journalists, writers and artists of this period recorded the truly appalling late Victorian London slums in graphic, heart-rending detail. In view of their revelations, it is questionable whether the street children who lived in such conditions were, in fact, any better off than their comrades who had no shelter at all. In the opening paragraphs of his article published in 1883, George Sims stated that 'no man who has seen "How the Poor Live" can return from the journey with aught but an aching heart.'[11] He pointed out that one slum was just like another and he encountered the following scene wherever his journey through the London slums took him.

> There is a monotony in the surroundings ... Rags, dirt, filth, wretchedness, the same figures, the same faces, the same old story of one room unfit for habitation yet inhabited by eight or nine people, the same complaint of a ruinous rent absorbing three-fourths of the toiler's weekly wage, the same shameful neglect by the owner of the property of all sanitary precautions, rotten floors, oozing walls, broken windows, crazy staircases, tile-less roofs, and in and around the dwelling-place of hundreds of honest citizens the nameless abominations which could only be set forth were we contributing to the Lancet instead of the Pictorial World – these are the things which confront us ...'[12]

Sims' readers must have been particularly horrified to read that dead bodies were sometimes left to rot for days in rooms inhabited by the living because of a lack of mortuaries in the slum districts and the inability of poor families to pay for funerals. Sims revealed that, as in the earlier period, the poor who were struggling to survive honestly were forced to live in these dreadful conditions alongside beggars, prostitutes and criminals, including murderers. As the following extract illustrates, Sims was deeply concerned about the impact this had on slum children.

> It is not only that crime and vice and disorder flourish luxuriantly in these colonies, through the dirt and discomfort bred of intemperance of the inhabitants, but the effect upon the children is terrible. The offspring of drunken fathers and mothers inherit not only a tendency to vice, but they come into the world physically and mentally unfit to conquer in life's battle. The wretched, stunted, mis-shapen child-object one comes upon in these localities, is the most painful part of our explorer's experience.[13]

Although horrified at the effects of drunkenness and the other vices of slum dwellers on their children, Sims did not condemn them. Instead, he blamed 'the shameful way in which they are housed, the callous neglect of their rights as citizens by the governing class ...' and remarked that they were 'entitled to the highest credit for not being twenty times more depraved than they are'.[14] It was blunt writing such as this which finally brought home the seriousness of the suffering of the London underclass and the knowledge that their plight could be ignored no longer.

In 1884 Andrew Mearns published *The Bitter Cry of Outcast London*, which reiterated the revelations of Sims and drew particular attention, in sensational language, to the lack of religious belief and immorality, including incest, prevalent among London's slum dwellers. He warned that 'this terrible flood of sin and misery is gaining upon us. It is rising every day.'[15] He pointed out that all the help provided by charities, missions, reformatories, refuges and temperance societies had touched 'only the merest edge of the great dark region of poverty, misery, squalor and immorality.'[16] This pamphlet led to an astonishing outcry in the press and, according to *Reynold's Newspaper,* caused 'a tremendous sensation and thrill of horror throughout the land.'[17] A national demand for urgent action on behalf of suffering slum dwellers soon followed. Tenniel's drawing 'Mammon's Rents', published in *Punch* at the height of the furore, summed up the feelings unleashed by the pamphlet. No doubt the reaction of the better-off classes contained an element of concern for themselves as well as for the suffering slum dwellers.

In the late 1880s Charles Booth embarked on his groundbreaking, detailed and comprehensive study of poverty, industry and religion in London, beginning with the East End district of Tower Hamlets. Booth was shocked to discover that 30 per cent of Londoners lived below his poverty line, meaning that they endured a hand-to-mouth existence of chronic want. Like Henry Mayhew, Booth emphasised that the poor could not be blamed for their plight, which was due to circumstances beyond their control such as sickness, unemployment or the casual, seasonal nature of their work. The first volumes of Booth's study were published in 1889, three years before the work of his namesake William Booth. The harrowing revelations of both men added to the growing evidence of London poverty and contributed to the demands for something to be done to help the poor.

The immediate response to this demand was an increase in charitable efforts, especially in the East End. Groups of university students arrived there to live among and help the poor, a practice referred to as 'slumming'. Money was also donated and a fund for the unemployed was set up by the Lord Mayor which raised a total of £78,000. A number of riots and demonstrations against unemployment in the 1880s and a strike of dock workers in 1889 added to tensions. Fears of social unrest and an uprising of those at the bottom of the social pyramid, which had receded somewhat since Mayhew and his contemporaries had stirred them up, resurfaced. The issues of poverty, unemployment and crime once again became subjects of public debate.

It was now clear that charitable and philanthropic efforts and the government's piecemeal response were no longer enough to deal with London's severe poverty and its associated social problems. The rise and growth of Socialism at this time was also significant. Socialists believed that the state should compel people to work together to overcome social problems. These factors finally forced the government, slowly and reluctantly, to abandon its policy of laissez-faire and intervene on a large scale. The findings of Charles Booth and the revelations of the later social investigative journalists had played a significant part in forcing the government to act. The abandonment of laissez-faire coincided with an increase in wages, a rise in living standards, a fall in food prices and a decline in the birth rate, which all helped to ease the plight of the poor.

A Royal Commission was set up in 1884 to investigate working-class housing and the East End Dwellings Company was founded in the same year, specifically to help the abject poor in that part of London. In 1888 the London County Council was established, assuming the responsibilities and functions of the Metropolitan Board of Works, and immediately set about the task of solving the problem of housing the poor. In 1890 the Housing of the Working Class Act was passed, making councils responsible for providing decent accommodation for the people in their locality. The advent of social housing soon followed; the first such housing in London was the Boundary Estate, which was built on the site of a notorious slum in Bethnal Green. At last the needs of 'outcast London' were being properly addressed and the beneficiaries included the slum dwellers among the later street children.

CHAPTER 15

Solving the Problem

Morning Assembly at a Board School

Just as at the large public schools of England the boys meet together for morning prayers, so in like fashion the day begins at the Kilburn Lane Higher Grade School ... First a hymn is sung, accompanied by the string band ... and by a youthful organist. This band is, all things considered, an excellent one, and its employment conduces greatly to the reverent interest taken by the boys in the proceedings. Prayers, read by the headmaster, follow, after which the scholars go to their respective class-rooms to enter upon the studies of the day.

A Board School Cookery Class

Twenty-four girls attending the Kilburn Lane School, all with neat pinafores on, form the class. Half of them ... are occupied in copying recipes while the other dozen are busily engaged in preparing various homely dishes suitable for an artisan's dinner. The expert teacher has spent the first hour of the morning in explaining how the work is to be done, and the young plain-cooks-in-the-making are now showing in practice how far they have mastered their lesson.

A Board School Carpentry Class

Cookery for the girls carpentry for the boys. Such is the programme carried out at the Kilburn Lane Higher Grade School ... Each boy in attendance receives weekly two-and-a-half hours instruction in practical woodwork, drawing, and the growth and structure of the different varieties of hard and soft wood. The lads are also taught how to grind and sharpen the tools they use. It is not at all astonishing that for most boys, whatever they may think of other lessons, this branch of elementary education has an irresistible attraction. The authorities are satisfied that such work fulfils its purpose, which is the training of the eyes and hands to habits of accuracy and neatness.

Extracts taken from Anon., *The Queen's London: a Pictorial and Descriptive Record of the Streets, Buildings, Parks and Scenery of the Great Metropolis*, 1896

In the 1840s Henry Mayhew had strongly advocated the education of London's street children as he believed that there was no future for them until this happened. This belief turned out to be correct, as it was the advent of state education in the later Victorian period which effectively solved the problem posed by the street children and ultimately provided a way forward for them. The changes brought about by state education also proved the wisdom of the belief held by Mayhew and others that the solution to poverty lay in helping the poor to help themselves.

The most obvious way in which the Education Acts solved the problem of London's street children was by taking them off the streets. This process gathered pace when education was made compulsory for children up to the age of ten in 1880 and continued when the school leaving age was raised to eleven in 1893 and twelve in 1899. However, as mentioned previously, for some time it was hard to enforce compulsory education because of the difficulties it caused to many poor parents who relied on the earnings of their children. George Sims described these difficulties in *How the Poor Live*:

> Few persons who have not actual experience of the lives of the poorest classes can have any conception of the serious import to them of the Education Act. Compulsory education is a national benefit. I am one of its stoutest defenders, but it is idle to deny that it is an Act which has gravely increased the burthens of the poor earning precarious livelihoods and as self-preservation is the first law of nature, there is small wonder that every dodge that craft and cunning can suggest is practised to evade it.[1]

Sims attended a meeting where parents had to explain their reasons for not sending their children to school and why they should not be summoned to appear before a magistrate for not doing so. The reasons given included the child not having any boots to wear to school, the inability to pay the school pence, and the child being needed at home to care for younger children and to help their overburdened mothers with household chores. The school boards and magistrates often showed sympathy and understanding towards parents in genuine difficulties and did their best to accommodate them. They provided boots for children and remitted the school fees in deserving cases until elementary school fees were abolished in 1891. They also granted permission for children to attend school half-time, once they had attained a certain educational standard, to enable them to work part-time or to carry out domestic responsibilities. However, the 'half-time' dispensation also posed problems, as George Sims bluntly explained:

> Many a lad whose thick skull keeps him from passing the standard which would leave him free to go to work, has a deft hand, strong arms and a broad back

– three things which fetch a fair price in the labour market.[2]

Despite the help extended to poor parents to make it easier for them to send their children to school, many teachers found themselves on the receiving end of parental wrath concerning this issue. It must also have been extremely difficult for self-supporting street children without parents to comply with the law by attending school.

As time passed the school authorities became much stricter about attendance. Attendance officers, called 'Visitors' in London, had the unenviable task of enforcing attendance. Police officers and mission and charity workers in the slum areas all helped by looking out for school-age children on the streets during school hours. Any homeless children who were discovered were found somewhere to live, often in a foster home. Many street children must have been discovered when the streets were scoured for truants. Attendance figures were used to calculate government grants to schools, which gave them an added incentive to be strict about truancy. Attendance registers were meticulously kept and figures were carefully recorded in school log books with detailed explanations for absences. Schools awarded prizes, medals and certificates to reward good attendance. Some schools recorded each child's attendance on elaborately decorated individual cards which were a source of great pride to many children. As a result of all these measures, average school attendance in England and Wales rose in twenty years from 10 to 90 per cent.[3] In 1891 state school education was made free, which helped many poor families.

The primary intention of state education was to create good citizens and prepare children for work fitting their station in life. As nearly all state school pupils were from the working classes, this meant educating them for lowly jobs. The future of the nation, including its ability to defend itself and to compete with other industrial nations, was also an important consideration. Before the aims of state education could be addressed, however, a large number of the children attending school for the first time had to be turned into decent, civilized human beings. The feral type of street child fell into this category. This was the first important step towards giving them a proper chance in life. Such middle-class values as cleanliness, tidiness, punctuality, diligence, gratitude, respect, truthfulness, obedience, dutifulness and good behaviour had to be instilled in children whose chaotic lives lacked order and structure. Many children had to be taught to sit still and be quiet. Instilling the basic requirement of cleanliness was particularly difficult. School log books reveal how frequently children were sent home to have a good wash in the early years of compulsory state education. Bad behaviour was recorded in a punishment book and dealt with by physical and other forms of punishment; good behaviour was encouraged by incentives and rewards.

Thomas Barnardo described how the School Board had 'brought education to the most neglected'[4] and how it had contributed to the 'silent but profound revolution'[5] which he noticed all around him in London in the last years of the century. Among the beneficiaries of this 'revolution' were the street children, as the following extract from Barnardo's memoirs illustrates:

> As I walk through the streets I see no more the organized beggary, the universally ingrained ignorance, the systematic neglect, the vicious exploiting of homeless little victims of cruelty and greed which disgraced London in the sixties. Of course I speak broadly. Alas, however, all is not "couleur de rose". There are still many wrongs to right; there is much wickedness to combat; the cry of the children still rises to the God of Saboath. But, as compared with the time when I first began my work, the law had broken with its evil traditions, and the spirit of apathy and laissez faire is beginning to die out. Behind the law is a rising level of public opinion and Christian sentiment, which means yet greater things in the future than in the past.[6]

The school curriculum placed great emphasis on the three Rs to provide a basic education. This was very successful as literacy rates increased rapidly until by 1900 97 per cent of children were literate.[7] Religious instruction was not compulsory in non-denominational London board schools but was often given. Physical education was provided in the form of drill lessons which, with their military overtones, were also used to instil and maintain discipline and obedience. Boys were taught practical vocational subjects such as woodwork and metalwork, to prepare them for future employment. Girls, meanwhile, were taught domestic subjects such as cookery, needlework, home economy and child-care to make them good housewives, mothers and domestic servants. The instruction received by girls played an important role in improving the lives of later generations of the London poor, as George Sims noted when he visited a school in 1883:

> Directly we enter we are struck with the appearance of these children. Bad faces there are among them – bruises and scars, and bandages and rags – but the bulk of these younger children have a generally *better* appearance than their little neighbours. There is a theory in the school, and it is borne out to a certain extent by fact, that some of the youngest and best-looking are the children of girls who just got the benefit of the Education Act before they were too old, and who in their young married life have reaped the benefit of those principles of cleanliness and thrift which the Board School inculcates. The young mothers are already a race far ahead of the older ones in this district and the children naturally benefit by it.[8]

The children benefiting from the Education Acts in this way included those who, without a board school education, may well have ended up on the streets as many of the previous generation did.

George Sims recognised that state education would be the 'prime instrument' in improving the lives of the poor. His visits to London board schools encouraged him to anticipate much brighter prospects for the young of the present and future generations. He confidently predicted that 'after years of discipline and culture' provided by the new state education system, poor children would 'go forth to lead lives which with their fathers and mothers were impossible.'[9] Job prospects for the poor, though still limited, were improved by state education, especially by the resulting improved literacy rates. Poor children were at last being provided with the basic skills and discipline to support themselves in a respectable, though lowly, job. The introduction of other subjects, such as geography and history, at the end of the century widened the horizons of poor children. The days had gone in which children, especially those who spent most of their lives on the streets, knew only what was necessary for their survival. State education provided poor children with a greater chance of escaping from poverty, although many were still held back by their home backgrounds.

The appalling physical condition of many poor children became evident in the 1880s when they attended school for the first time. Until then there was very little knowledge about the health of the country's poorest children. Many of the new board school children turned up severely malnourished, weak, ill, dirty, flea-bitten, verminous, inadequately dressed and barefoot. Some London head teachers, as elsewhere in the country, provided charity-funded food for pupils too hungry to concentrate on lessons. In 1882 the London School Board Free Dinner Fund was set up, and in 1888 the Free Breakfast and Dinner Fund was established by the headmistress of a school in Southwark and the writer George Sims. By the end of the century a considerable number of the capital's schoolchildren benefited from these initiatives. Nevertheless, when recruitment for the Boer War began in 1899 it became clear that much was still needed to be done to improve the physical condition of the young.

Further research into poverty added to the growing pressure on the government to intervene in the lives of the poor. A Royal Commission on Labour in 1885 and a study of the city of York by Seebohm Rowntree in 1903 both confirmed the findings of Charles Booth on poverty. Legislation was finally passed to help the poor, including children, by the Liberal government which came to power in 1906. State schools were the means by which much of this legislation was delivered and state control over the lives of poor children was effected. A School Meals Act was passed in 1906, allowing local authorities to provide meals for children paid for by a levy on the rates; this later became compulsory. In 1907 the Schools Medical Inspection Service was introduced to provide annual medicals for all state schoolchildren. In London, medical treatment was also provided. Children in other state-run or regulated institutions for poor children received the same level of state control in their lives. The state was now firmly involved in the lives of poor children, who became in effect the 'children of the state'. The nation, therefore, had an interest in their health and well-being and a duty to ensure they were nurtured and cared for properly.

In 1908 the Children's Act, also known as the Children's and Young Person's Act, was passed by the reforming Liberal government to consolidate and extend legislation to protect children. Under this Act further offences of child neglect were added to those of child cruelty and local authorities were given powers to keep poor children out of the workhouse and protect them from abuse, including taking them away from their homes. Further restrictions were placed on child employment and children were banned from buying cigarettes and entering pubs. Juvenile courts were set up so that children could be dealt with separately from adults and Borstals were built for young offenders. The role of the courts was now to rescue as well as to punish children. The state could now force parents to fulfill their responsibilities and step in to supply the deficiencies of inadequate parenting.

As a result of the new legislation, poor children were finally able to enjoy a defined period of their lives when they could be children, like their better-off peers. The right of all children to reasonable treatment was finally acknowledged and enshrined in law, their welfare was attended to and they could spend their early years being educated and prepared to start adult life at an appropriate age instead of being pushed into it prematurely. Even though many children were still expected to help in the home and contribute any earnings to the family coffers, they had been relieved of at least some of their responsibilities.

Although some children managed to slip through the new state safety net, the majority of poor children, including those who otherwise may well have ended up on the streets, were at last cared for and protected. The blight of neglected, abandoned and unwanted children struggling to survive on the streets of the capital of a great and rich empire had been largely removed. Furthermore, as indicated by the new, kinder names used to describe children of the underclass, they were no longer perceived as a threat to society. In fact, the threat of 'outcast London', of which the street children had formed a significant part, turned out to be no more than a threat. It had never materialised into anything more substantial.

By the Edwardian period large numbers of poor children spending most of their lives on the streets of London and other cities had become a thing of the past. They were now to be found in school or at home, either the family home, a rescue home or one provided by the state. The prospects of such children, though limited in comparison with those higher up the social scale, would have seemed unthinkable to the street children whose plight was revealed by Henry Mayhew and his fellow journalists in the early years of Victoria's reign. A new era had dawned for the children of the poor.

Notes

1. Setting the Scene

1. Friedrich Engels, *The Condition of the Working Classes in England,* p. 59.
2. Henry Mayhew and John Binny, *The Criminal Prisons of London and Scenes of Prison Life,* p. 9.

2. The Early Social Investigative Journalists and Writers

1. Christopher Hibbert, *The English, A Social History,* p. 627.
2. Charles Dickens, *Shops and Tenants, Sketches by Boz.*
3. Charles Dickens, Letter to Mrs Elizabeth Gaskell, 31.1.1850.
4. Peter Quennell, *Mayhew's Characters,* p. xvii.
5. Ibid, p. xix.
6. John Hollingshead, *Ragged London in 1861,* p. 117.
7. Ibid, p. 2.

3. Who Were the Street Children?

1. Henry Mayhew, *London Labour and the London Poor,* Neuburg edition, p. 162.
2. Ibid, p. 162.
3. *Punch,* 'Street Arabs', July to December 1842.
4. John Pollock, *Shaftesbury the Reformer,* p. 73.
5. Anna Davin, *Growing up Poor,* pp. 162–3.
6. Henry Mayhew, *London Labour and the London Poor,* p. 185.
7. Ibid, p. 181.

4. Scratching a Living: Selling and Finding

1. Ben Weinreb and Christopher Hibbert, *The London Encyclopedia*, p. 956.
2. Mayhew, *London Labour and the London Poor*, p. 65.
3. Ibid, p. 65.
4. Ibid, p. 64.
5. Ibid, p. 68.
6. Ibid, p. 65.
7. Ibid, p. 65.
8. Ibid, p. 66.
9. Ibid, p. 61.
10. Ibid, p. 63.
11. Ibid, p. 123.
12. Ibid, p. 124.
13. Ibid, p. 124.
14. Ibid, p. 125.
15. Ibid, p. 210.
16. Ibid, p. 211.
17. Ibid, p. 211.
18. Ibid, p. 211.
19. Ibid, p. 215.
20. Ibid, p. 215
21. Ibid, p. 216.
22. Ibid, pp. 217–8.
23. Ibid, p. 218.

5. Street Entertainers and Labourers

1. Mayhew, *London Labour and the London Poor*, p. 320.
2. Ibid, p. 324.
3. Max Schlesinger, *Saunterings In and Around London*, extract 33.
4. Mayhew, p. 278.
5. Ibid, p. 280.
6. Ibid, p. 281.
7. Ibid, p. 281.
8. Ibid, p. 330
9. Ibid, p. 334.
10. Anon, 'London Fogs and London Poor', *Continental Magazine,* October 1862.
11. Ibid.
12. Arthur Munby, *Diary 1862.*
13. Mayhew, p. 289.
14. Ibid, p. 289.

15. Ibid, p. 290.

16. Ibid, p. 291.

17. Ibid, p. 291.

18. Ibid, p. 277.

19. Ibid, p. 277.

20. Adolphe Smith and John Thomson, *Victorian London Street Life*, p. 131.

21. Ibid, 134.

22. James Ewing Ritchie, *Here and There in London*.

23. Ibid.

24. Ibid.

25. Mayhew, p. 38

26. Ibid, p. 37

27. Ibid, p. 41.

6. Criminal Children

1. Henry Mayhew, *The Morning Chronicle Survey of Labour and the Poor; The Metropolitan Districts*, vol. 4, pp. 37–8.

2. James Greenwood, *The Seven Curses of London*, p. 2.

3. Thomas Archer, *The Terrible Sights of London*, p. 216.

4. Greenwood, p. 125.

5. Ibid, p. 126.

6. Ibid, p. 126.

7. Peter Quennell, *London's Underworld*, p. 217.

8. Jeannie Duckworth, *Fagin's Children*, p. 15.

9. Mayhew, *The Morning Chronicle of Labour and the Poor; The Metropolitan Districts*, vol. 4, p. 42.

10. James Greenwood, p. 129.

11. Charles Dickens, *Sketches by Boz, A Visit to Newgate*, Neil Philip and Victor Neuburg, *Charles Dickens A December Vision and Other Thoughtful Writings*, p. 59.

12. Duckworth, p. 9.

13. Quennell, *London's Underworld*, p. 241.

14. Charles Dickens, *Reprinted Pieces*, p. 174.

15. Ibid, p. 174.

16. Mayhew, letter dated 25.1.1850, *The Morning Chronicle Survey of Labour and the Poor; The Metropolitan Districts*, vol. 3, p. 50.

17. Mayhew, *London Labour and the London Poor*, p. 373.

18. Archer, p. 233.

19. Quennell, *London's Underworld*, p. 214.

20. Ibid, p. 228.

21. Ibid, p. 300.

22. Ibid, p. 303.

23. Ibid, p. 304.

24. Archer, p. 213.

25. Mayhew and Binny, *The Criminal Prisons of London and Scenes of Prison Life*, p. 471.

26. Mayhew, *Letter to The Morning Chronicle, The Morning Chronicle Survey of Labour and the Poor; the Metropolitan Districts*, vol. 3, p. 102.

27. Ibid, p. 102.

28. Dickens, *A Visit to Newgate, Sketches by Boz,* Neil and Neuburg, p. 61.

29. Mayhew, *Letter to The Morning Chronicle 14.3.1850, The Morning Chronicle Survey of Labour and the Poor, The Metropolitan Districts*, vol. 4, p. 34.

30. See Duckworth, chapters 12–13 on reformatories and industrial schools.

7. Child Prostitutes

1. Flora Tristan, *The London Journal of Flora Tristan*, p. 83.

2. Peter Quennell, *London's Underworld*, p. 43.

3. W. O'Daniel, *Ins and Outs of London*.

4. Mayhew, Letter to The Morning Chronicle, *The Morning Chronicle Survey of Labour and the Poor: The Metropolitan Districts*, vol. 1, p. 231.

5. Mayhew, *London Labour and the London Poor*, p. 437.

6. Fyodor Dostoevsky, *Winter Notes on Summer Impressions,* extract in Jon Lewis, *London The Autobiography*, pp. 258–9.

7. W. O'Daniel, extract 5.

8. Mayhew, *London Labour and the London Poor*, p. 475.

9. Charles Dickens, *The Prisoners' Van, Sketches by Boz,* Rosalind Vallance, *Dickens' London*, p. 85.

10. Ibid, p. 86.

11. Ibid, p. 86.

12. Ibid, p. 86.

13. Mayhew, letter to The Morning Chronicle 13.11.1849, *The Morning Chronicle Survey of Labour and the Poor: The Metropolitan Districts* vol. 1, p. 151.

14. Archer, pp. 474–5.

8. A Place to Sleep: The Homes of the Street Children

1. Hollingshead, p. 7.

2. Tristan, p. 155.

3. Ibid, p. 156.

4. Ibid, pp. 157–8.

5. George Godwin, *London Shadows, A Glance at the "Homes" of the Thousands,* p. 11.

6. Gavin Weightman and Steve Humphries, *The Making of Modern London*, p. 113.

7. Francis Sheppard, *London 1808–1870, The Infernal Wen*, p. 292.

8. Mayhew, *London Labour and the London Poor*, p. 113.

9. Ibid, p. 114.

10. Jerry White, *London in the Nineteenth Century, A Human Awful Wonder of God*, p. 331.

11. Engels, p. 66.

12. Mayhew, *London Labour and the London Poor*, p. 422.

13. Ibid, p. 418.

14. Sheppard, p. 379.

15. Ibid, p. 379.

16. James Grant, *Sketches in London*, p. 245.

17. Sheppard, p. 382.

18. Mayhew, *London Labour and the London Poor*, p. 411.

19. Peter Keating, *Into Unknown England 1866–1913, Selections from the Social Explorers*, p. 37.

20. Charles Dickens, *A Nightly Scene in London, Household Words*, 26.1.1856.

21. Grant, p. 230.

22. Archer, p. 279.

9. Helping the Street Children

1. Pamela Horn, *The Victorian Town Child*, p. 184.

2. Francis Sheppard, p. 380.

3. George Sims, *How the Poor Live*, p. 54.

4. Ewing Ritchie, *About London*, p. 78.

5. E. P. Thompson and Eileen Yeo, *The Unknown Mayhew*, p. 46.

6. Sheppard, p. 384.

7. Thompson and Yeo, p. 36.

8. Gustave Doré and Blanchard Jerrold, *London A Pilgrimage*, p. 151.

9. See Frank Prochaska, *Women and Philanthropy in Nineteenth Century England*, pp. 5–7, on the philanthropic role of middle-class women.

10. Irene Howat and John Nicholls, *Streets Paved With Gold*, p. 32.

11. William Locke, *Evidence to the Select Committee on Criminal and Destitute Juveniles*, 1852.

12. Howat and Nicholls, p. 81.

13. Anon., *A Glance at Field Lane Ragged School, The Leisure Hour*, 1858.

14. Archer, p. 287.

15. Ibid, p. 287.

16. Mrs Barnardo and James Marchant, *Memoirs of the Late Dr Barnardo*, p. 86.

17. Archer, p. 188.

18. Roger J. Owen, *The National Children's Home*, p. 7.

19. Ibid, p. 7.

20. Ethel Hogg, *Quintin Hogg, A Biography*, p. 55.

21. Charles Dickens, *Crime and Education, Daily News*, 4.2.1846, Philip and Neuburg, p. 93.

22. William Locke, *Evidence to the Select Committee on Criminal and Destitute Children*, 1852.

23. Archer, p. 240.

24. Mayhew, *Letter to The Morning Chronicle, 25.4.1850, The Morning Chronicle Survey of Labour and the Poor; The Metropolitan Districts*, vol. 4, pp. 131–153.

25. Archer, p. 234.

26. *See* www.redhill-reigate-history.co uk/philanth.htm for the history of the Royal Philanthropic Society.

27. Duckworth, pp. 186–7 and p. 231.

28. Report of the trial of J. Jacobs at Middlesex Sessions, *The Times*, 3.3.1837.

29. Letter to *The Times*, 23.12.1864.

10. The Changing Scene

1. Richard Rowe, *Life in the London Streets or Struggles for Daily Bread*, p. 106.

2. Hugh Clout, *The Times History Atlas*, p. 98.

3. Sheppard, p. 150.

11. The Later Social Investigative Journalists and Other Writers

1. Gustave Doré and Blanchard Jerrold, p. 1.

2. Ibid, p. 2.

3. Rowe, p. iii.

4. Sims, p. 5.

5. Ibid, p. 10.

6. Keating, p. 94.

7. Ibid, pp. 103–4.

8. Ibid, p. 92.

9. Ibid, p. 93.

10. William Booth, *In Darkest England and the Way Out*, p. 18.

11. Ibid, p. 21.

12. Surviving on the Streets

1. Thomas Wright, *The Great Army of the London Poor*, p. 280.
2. Richard Rowe, *Life in the London Street; or Struggles for Daily Bread*, pp. 240–1.
3. Ibid, p. 247.
4. Ibid, p. 248.
5. Ibid, p. 248
6. D. Rice-Jones, *In the Slums*, p. 111.
7. Ibid, p. 111.
8. Ibid, p. 112.
9. Ibid, p. 112.
10. Barnardo and Marchant, p. 158.
11. Ibid, p. 158.
12. Ibid, p. 159.
13. Rowe, *Episodes in an Obscure Life*, p. 76.
14. Thomas Wright, *The Great Army of the London Poor*, p. 283.
15. Ibid, p. 287.
16. Ibid, p. 290.
17. Duckworth, p. 235.
18. Rowe, *Life in the London Streets; or Struggles for Daily Bread*, p. 225.
19. Ibid, p. 233.
20. Ibid, p. 235.
21. Ibid, p. 236.

13. Helping the Later Street Children

1. Barnardo and Marchant, p. 154.
2. Ibid, p. 154.
3. Ibid, p. 228.
4. Ibid, p. 207.
5. Ibid, p. 325.
6. Cyril Davey, *A Man For All Children, The Story of Thomas Bowman Stephenson*, p. 56.
7. Waifs and Strays Society, *A Chronicle of the Church of England's Waifs and Strays Society 1808–1920*, pp. 84–5.
8. 'Uncle Jonathan', *Street Arabs, Walks In and Around London*.
9. Barnardo and Marchant, p. 324.
10. Pamela Horn, *Children's Work and Welfare, 1780–1880s*, pp. 88.
11. Horn, *The Victorian Town Child*, p. 208.
12. Horn, *Children's Work and Welfare, 1780–1880s*, pp. 88.

14. Homes of the Later Street Children

1. Booth, p. 34.
2. Ibid, p. 38.
3. Rowe, *Life in the London Streets: or Struggles for Daily Bread*, p. 164.
4. Ibid, pp. 165–6.
5. Ibid, pp. 166–7.
6. Ibid, p. 166.
7. Ibid, p. 165.
8. Rowe, *Episodes in an Obscure Life*, p. 71.
9. White, p. 331.
10. Booth, p. 76.
11. George Sims, *How the Poor Live*, p. 5.
12. Ibid, p. 29.
13. Ibid, p. 15.
14. Ibid, p. 55.
15. Keating, p. 92.
16. Ibid, p. 92.
17. Weightman and Humphries, p. 169.

15. Solving the Problem

1. Sims, p. 19.
2. Ibid, p. 19.
3. Trevor May, *The Victorian Schoolroom*, p. 29.
4. Barnardo and Marchant, p. 243.
5. Ibid, p. 244.
6. Ibid, p. 243.
7. James Walvin, *A Child's World, A History of English Childhood 1800–1914*, p. 121.
8. Sims, p. 32.
9. Ibid, p. 32.

Biographies

of those whose work has been used as sources and other people who feature in the story of the street children

Thomas Archer
Clergyman, Social Investigator and Author

All that can be discovered about Thomas Archer is that he investigated the lives of the London poor, especially children, and described his findings in *The Pauper, The Thief and The Convict* (1865) and *The Terrible Sights of London* (1870).

Reference has also been found to his authorship of *Wayfe Summer* and *Madame Prudence*.

Thomas Barnardo
Doctor, Philanthropist and Founder of Barnardo's Children's Homes

Thomas John Barnardo was born in Dublin in July 1845, the son of a furrier. As a young man Barnardo worked and preached among the poor in the slums of Dublin before moving to London to train as a doctor at the London Hospital, Whitechapel. Barnardo's intention was to become a medical missionary in China. He began his work with the London poor by teaching in ragged schools. In 1867 he founded the East End Juvenile Mission.

When Barnardo learned about the huge numbers of homeless and destitute children in London, he gave up his ambition of going to China and devoted his life to rescuing 'nobody's children'. He opened his first home in Stepney Causeway in 1870.

In 1873 Barnardo extended his work to include girls, babies, and disabled children. During his lifetime Dr Barnardo helped a quarter of a million children. After his death in September 1905, a memorial was erected to him near his village home for girls in Barkingside, Essex.

Catherine Booth
Co-founder of the Salvation Army

Catherine Booth, neé Mumford, was born in January 1829 in Ashbourne, Derby, the daughter of a Wesleyan preacher. A member of the Band of Hope and a supporter of the Temperance Movement, she married William Booth, a Methodist minister in 1855.

Booth was a gifted preacher and became involved in her husband's evangelical work. In 1865 they founded the Christian Mission, which became the Salvation Army in 1878. Catherine Booth started the army's women's work and came to be known as The Mother of the Army. She was the author of a number of books and leaflets including *Female Ministry*(1870). Catherine Booth died in October 1890.

Charles Booth
Businessman, Statistician and Social Reformer

Charles Booth was born in March 1840 in Liverpool, the son of a ship owner and corn merchant. He was educated at the Royal Institution School in Liverpool before going into business with his brother in the leather industry. They founded the Booth Steamship Company together.

Booth moved to London in 1875 and became familiar with the capital's poverty when he took to walking around the slum districts. His groundbreaking study of the London poor was published between 1889 and 1903.

Booth became President of the Royal Statistical Society in 1882, a fellow of the Royal Society in 1899 and a Privy Councillor in 1904. He died in November 1916.

William Booth
Methodist Minister and Co-Founder of the Salvation Army

William Booth was born in Nottingham in 1829, the son of a builder. After converting to Christianity he became a Methodist preacher. Booth moved to London in 1849 and married Catherine Mumford in 1855. They founded the London Christian Mission in 1865 and began their work among the London poor. The Mission became the Salvation Army in 1878, a religious movement which spread worldwide. The Salvation Army provided practical help for the poor as well as spiritual comfort.

Booth's book *In Darkest England and the Way Out* was published in 1892. He was made a Freeman of the City of London and was awarded an honorary degree by Oxford University.

Booth died in August 1912, when his son William Bramwell Booth took over as General of the Salvation Army.

Angela Burdett-Coutts
Philanthropist

Angela Burdett-Coutts was born in April 1814. She was the daughter of Francis Burdett, the Radical MP, and the grand-daughter of Thomas Coutts, the banker whose fortune she inherited.

Burdett-Coutts spent her inheritance money on helping those in need, especially the poor of East London. Her philanthropic work included founding a home for fallen women, building model homes for the poor, a market selling cheap food, churches, schools, missions and hospitals. She was also a patron of the arts.

In 1871 Burdett-Coutts was the first woman to be made a baroness in her own right and in 1872 she became the first woman to receive the freedom of the city of London. She died in 1906.

Charles Dickens
Novelist, Journalist, Essayist and Editor

Charles John Huffam Dickens was born in Landport, Portsmouth in February 1812, the son of a clerk in the Naval Pay Office. The Dickens family moved to London when he was twelve. Soon afterwards, Charles and his older sister were left to fend for themselves when their father was imprisoned for debt. During this time Dickens worked in a blacking factory. He received some schooling on his father's release from prison.

Dickens was a clerk in a solicitor's office before becoming a short-hand court reporter. In 1832 he started work as a reporter in the House of Commons for the *Mirror of Parliament* and *The Morning Chronicle*. Dickens contributed to monthly magazines using the pseudonyms of Boz and Tibbs. His career as a novelist began with the serialization of *The Pickwick Papers* in 1836. He founded and edited the periodicals *Master Humphrey's Clock, Household Words* and *All the Year Round*. Dickens died in June 1870.

Gustave Doré
Artist, Engraver, Illustrator and Sculptor

Gustave Doré was born in Strasbourg in January 1832, the son of an engineer. He began drawing as a young child. He illustrated the works of many authors, including Rabelais, Balzac, Milton and Shakespeare, and a new edition of the Bible in 1866. Doré's work was also featured in the *Illustrated London News.* He held a major exhibition in London in 1867 and the Doré Gallery was opened in Bond Street soon after. In 1869 Doré collaborated with Blanchard Jerrold on *London; A Pilgrimage,* which was illustrated with 180 of his engravings. His work has been used to illustrate many books on Victorian London. Doré died in 1883.

Fyodor Dostoevsky
Russian Novelist

Fyodor Dostoevsky was born in Moscow in 1822, the son of an army surgeon. He studied engineering and spent three years in the army before embarking on his career as a novelist. Dostoevsky was sent to Siberia for three months for his political associations.

His *Winter Notes on Summer Impressions* was written following a visit to England. Dostoevsky's novels included *Crime and Punishment* (1866) and *The Brothers Karamazov* (1880). He died in February 1883.

Friedrich Engels
German Socialist and Writer

Friedrich Engels was born in Barmen, Prussia in November 1820. He moved to England as a young man to run his father's cotton factory in Manchester. His book *The Condition of the Working Classes in England,* about the poverty in London and England's industrial cities, was published in 1844. Engels became friendly with the leaders of the Chartist movement.

Engels collaborated with Karl Marx on *The Communist Manifesto,* published in 1848. He edited and translated Marx's work following his death in 1883. Engels died in August 1895.

George Godwin
Architect, Surveyor, Author and Editor

George Godwin was born in January 1815, the son of a builder. He entered the family practice at the age of thirteen. In 1835 he received the first medal awarded by the R.I.B.A. for an essay on concrete. He helped found, and was secretary for, the Art Union of London and wrote for a number of art and architectural journals.

Godwin belonged to the Institute of British Architects, the Society of Antiquaries and was a Fellow of the Royal Society. From 1834 to 1883 he was editor of

The Builder. He wrote about the London slums and campaigned for an improvement in the living conditions of the working classes.

As an architect Godwin worked on churches, houses, public houses and public buildings. Large parts of South Kensington and Earls Court were designed by him. He wrote a number of books on architecture. Godwin died in 1883.

James Grant
Newspaper Editor and Historian

James Grant was born in 1802. In 1827 he helped to found the *Elgin Courier*, which he edited until 1833. After moving to London, Grant wrote for *The Morning Chronicle* and *Morning Advertiser* and founded two journals of his own. In 1872 he became editor of the *Christian Standard*.

Grant's many books included *The Great Metropolis* (1837), *Sketches in London* (1838) and *Lights and Shadows of London Life* (1842). Grant died in 1879.

James Greenwood
Social Explorer, Journalist and Writer

James Greenwood was born in London between 1830 and 1835, the son of a coach-maker. He began his career writing for the *London Gazette* and wrote a number of articles and books drawing attention to the plight of the London poor. In 1866 he disguised himself as a vagrant in order to investigate life in a casual ward from the inside. His findings were revealed in *A Night in the Workhouse* (1866).

Greenwood's books included *Unsentimental Journeys: Byways of the Modern Babylon* (1867), *The Seven Curses of Victorian London* (1869) and *Low Life Deeps* (1876). He also wrote novels and short stories. Greenwood died in August 1927.

Octavia Hill
Philanthropist and Co-Founder of the National trust

Octavia Hill was born in Wisbech, Cambridgeshire in December 1838, the daughter of an unsuccessful banker. She was educated at home.

Hill founded the Charity Organisation Society in 1870 and, with the financial backing of William Ruskin, bought and improved slum homes for the working classes. She co-founded the National Trust in 1885 to preserve open spaces and buildings of historical interest. Her published works included *Homes of the London Poor* (1875) and *Our Common Land* (1877). Octavia Hill died in August 1912.

Quintin Hogg
Merchant and Philanthropist

Quintin Hogg was born in London in February 1845, the fourteenth child of Sir James Hogg. He was educated at Eton and made a fortune as a tea merchant.

In 1864 Hogg opened the Off Alley Ragged School in the Strand and in 1882 bought a lease on the Polytechnic Institution in Regent Street, which he opened as a Christian youth and education centre. Hogg's philanthropy was motivated by his Christian faith. He died in January 1903.

John Hollingshead
Journalist, Writer and Theatre Manager

John Hollingshead was born in London in September 1827. He began his career as a journalist by writing for *Household Words* and *Cornhill* magazine.

In 1861 Hollingshead became Special Correspondent for the *Morning Post*. He wrote a series of articles about the London poor which were later published as *Ragged London* (1861) and a series of political articles on the subject of social reform for *Punch*.

Hollingshead became stage director of the Alhambra Theatre from 1865 to 1868, when he became manager of the Gaiety Theatre. He wrote a number of plays and books about the theatre. He died in October 1904.

Henry Mayhew
Social Investigator, Journalist, Novelist and Playwright

Henry Mayhew was born in London in November 1812, the son of Joshua Mayhew, a lawyer. At the age of twelve, while at Westminster School, he ran way to sea. On his return he was articled to his father for three years before becoming a journalist.

Mayhew was co-founder of the weekly paper *Figaro in London* and wrote for the journal *The Thief*. In 1841 he founded *Punch* magazine with Mark Lemon. When the magazine was sold due to the inability to cover costs, Mayhew remained as 'suggester-in-chief'. When his railway magazine *The Iron Times* also failed, he was made bankrupt.

In 1849 Mayhew visited Bermondsey during a devastating cholera epidemic and wrote about the terrible sights he witnessed. He suggested to the editor on *The Morning Chronicle* the idea of investigating and reporting on the condition of the labouring classes in England and Wales. The idea was accepted and Mayhew became the London reporter, leading a team of investigators. His articles made a great impact on the middle-class reading public. These articles were later published in book form under the title *London Labour and the London Poor.*

In 1856 Mayhew embarked on another series of articles called *The Great World of London.* The crime articles in this series, written in collaboration with and completed by John Binny, became *The Criminal Prisons of London and Scenes of Prison Life*, published in 1862. Mayhew also wrote fairy tales, popular fiction and novels, some in collaboration with his brother Augustus.

Although Mayhew's articles on the poor made a great impact in the 1840s and early 1850s, he was largely forgotten when he died in July 1887.

Andrew Mearns
Congregational Minister and Author

Andrew Mearns was born in July 1837 in Burnside, Ayrshire. After a short spell as a teacher, Mearns trained for the ministry and became minister of the Congregational Church of Great Marlow and then, in 1866, of the New Congregational Church in Markham Square, Chelsea. He eventually gave up active ministry to become secretary of the London Congregational Union, a position he held until his retirement.

In 1883 Mearns started an inquiry into the conditions of London's slum dwellers and published his pamphlet *The Bitter Cry of Outcast London.* This led to a great outcry and resulted in the establishment of more Church missions in the East End, the work of the settlement movement and the setting up of a Royal Commission to investigate the issue of working-class housing. Mearns retired in 1906 and died in August 1925.

Arthur Munby
Lawyer, Poet and Diarist

Arthur Munby was born in August 1828 in York. After training as a lawyer he spent most of his working life as a civil servant in the Ecclesiastical Commissioner's Office.

Munby had an obsessive fascination for working-class women, especially those engaged in dirty, physical work. He spent a lot of time wandering around the streets of London and other cities, observing and interviewing such women. His observations were recorded in his diaries. Munby was briefly married to Hannah Cullwick, a maid he met on his travels. He died in January 1910.

James Payn
Novelist and Editor

Payn was born in 1830 in Cheltenham. He studied at Trinity College, Cambridge, and contributed to a number of journals and magazines including *Household Words, Chambers Journal* and *The Illustrated London News.* He became editor of *Cornhill Magazine* in 1883. Payn was a prolific writer of novels, short stories and essays. He died in London in 1898.

George Peabody
American Businessman, Banker and Philanthropist

George Peabody was born in February 1795 in South Danvers, Massachusetts. He earned a fortune as a partner in a dry goods store in Baltimore.

Peabody came to London in 1837 and established himself as a merchant and banker. He used his fortune to help the London poor and to build housing in London for working men. Peabody died in November 1869.

D. Rice-Jones
Church Minister and Author

D. Rice-Jones had a Master of Arts degree from Oxford University and worked as a London Diocesan Home Missionary.

He was author of *From Cellar to Garret* (date unknown) and *In the Slums* (1884).

Richard Rowe
Writer and Journalist

Richard Rowe was born in Doncaster in March 1828, the son of a Methodist minister. Rowe spent some time in Australia as a young man, where he began his career by writing articles for the press and publishing poetry. On his return to England he worked as a journalist and published a number of stories for children.

Rowe researched the lives of London's poor and used his findings to write *Episodes in an Obscure Life* (1871) and *Life in the London Streets: or Struggles for Daily Bread* (1871). He died in December 1879.

Edward Rudolf
Co-Founder of the Waifs and Strays Society

Edward de Montjoie Rudolf was born in London in April 1852, the son of a retired major. He started work at the age of thirteen as an office boy and then became a junior clerk at the Netherlands Consulate. Rudolf studied in the evenings to improve his education. In 1871 he passed the Civil Service exam and started work at the Office of Works in Whitehall.

In the same year Rudolf became Sunday School Superintendent at St Anne's church in Lambeth and became involved with the lives of the poor people of the parish. This work made him aware of the needs of London's homeless and destitute children and led to his founding the Waifs and Strays Society with his brother, in 1881. Eventually, this work became Rudolf's full time occupation. He died in 1933.

Robert Rudolf
Co-Founder of the Waifs and Strays Society

Robert de Montjoie Rudolf was born in 1856, the younger brother of Edward Rudolf. He worked with his brother as a clerk in the Netherlands Consulate and helped him to run the Sunday School at St Anne's church, Lambeth.

Rudolf co-founded the Waifs and Strays Society with Edward in 1881 and helped to run the society until his death in 1932.

Lord Shaftesbury
Philanthropist, MP and Social Reformer

Anthony Ashley Cooper, 7th Earl of Shaftesbury, was born in in April 1801. An evangelical Christian, Sabbatarian and Millenialist, Shaftesbury's philanthropy was motivated by his beliefs and a desire to save souls. He was MP for Woodstock, Dorchester and Dorset successively between 1826 and 1846. He was appointed Lord of the Admiralty in 1834 and succeeded to the earldom in 1851.

Shaftesbury agitated for reform in the treatment of lunatics and worked for 'nobody's people', as he called them, all his life. His long fight on behalf of factory workers, including children, led to the Ten Hours Act of 1847 and his campaign to help women and child mine workers led to the 1842 Mines Act.

In the 1840s Shaftesbury became involved in helping London's slum dwellers and destitute children. He became President of the Ragged School Union in 1846 and helped to spread the influence of ragged schools across the United Kingdom.

Shaftesbury died in October 1885 and the streets of London were lined with poor people as his funeral procession passed on its way to Westminster Abbey.

George Sims
Social Investigator, Journalist, Novelist, Playwright and Editor

George Sims was born in London in September 1847, the son of a businessman. His grandfather was the Chartist leader John Dinsmore Stevenson, who helped to form his political views.

Sims began his writing career as a theatre reviewer and wrote for a number of magazines and newspapers, including the *Weekly Dispatch* and the *Referee*. Sims adopted the pseudonym of Dagonet, under which he wrote poems on social issues. He also wrote a number of articles on social issues, including the living conditions of the London poor. The latter were later published in book form as *How the Poor Live* (1889) and *Horrible London* (1889).

Sims appeared as a witness before the Commission on Working Class Housing in 1884. He co-founded a charity which provided dinners for poor children in London.

His many literary works included the novel *Rogues and Vagabonds* (1885) and the play *The Lights of London (1881)*. His final work was his autobiography, *My Life: Sixty Years of Recollections of Bohemian London*. He died in September 1922.

Charles Spurgeon
Preacher and Founder of Stockwell Orphanage

Charles Haddon Spurgeon was born in June 1834 in Essex, the son of an Independent Church lay preacher. He worked briefly as a schoolmaster before becoming pastor of a Baptist chapel in Waterbeach, Cambridgeshire at the age of only eighteen.

Spurgeon moved two years later to Park Street Chapel in Southwark. He was a skilled orator who drew such large crowds to his services that he had to move to Exeter Hall in the Strand, and then to the music hall in Surrey Gardens. He also held open-air services.

Spurgeon raised money to build the Metropolitan Tabernacle near Elephant and Castle in 1861.He preached there to congregations of up to 5,000 people. His sermons were published.

As well as Stockwell Orphanage, which he founded in 1867, Spurgeon established a college for training Baptist ministers and some almshouses. Spurgeon died in January 1892.

William Stead
Journalist, Editor and Social Campaigner

William Stead was born in Embleton, Durham in July 1849, the son of a Congregational Church minister. He began his career as a journalist on the *Northern Echo* and became its editor at the age of twenty-two. He was assistant editor of the *Pall Mall Gazette* from 1880 to 1883, and its editor from 1883 to 1890, when he moved on to found the *Review of Reviews*. Stead claimed to be the founder of the 'New Journalism', the fore-runner of the popular press of the twentieth century.

Stead had a strong Puritan faith and campaigned on a number of social issues and causes, including juvenile prostitution, criminal law amendment and peace. He had many interests, including spiritualism, and was the author of a number of books on political and other subjects.

Stead died on his way to America in April 1812 when the *Titanic*, on which he was a passenger, sunk after hitting an iceberg.

Thomas Bowman Stephenson
Wesleyan Methodist Minister and Founder of the National Children's Home and Orphanage, London

Stephenson was born in Newcastle-on-Tyne in December 1839, the son of a Wesleyan minister. He trained as a Methodist minister and worked in a number of churches before being appointed to the chapel in Waterloo Road, Lambeth in 1868.

With the help of Alfred Mager and Francis Horner, Stephenson opened a children's home in Lambeth in 1869 and became its principal in 1873. This was the first of a number of homes and was the beginning of the National Children's Homes. Stephenson pioneered the training of people working with children. He founded the Order of the Sisters of the Children and the Wesleyan Deaconess Order. He also set up a children's home in Ontario in 1873.

In 1900 Stephenson gave up his position of principal of the London home and became a minister in Ilkley and warden of the Deaconess Institution, which relocated there.

He retired in 1907 and returned to London, where he died in 1912. At the time of his death there were 2,201 children in the care of the National Children's Home and Orphanage and 229 Wesleyan Deaconesses.

Hippolyte Taine
French Historian, Critic and Academic

Hippolyte Taine was born in Vouziers, Ardennes, in April 1828, the son of a lawyer. He became Professor of Aesthetics at the École des Beaux-Arts in 1862. Taine was the author of a number of books on French history and philosophy. His book *Notes on England* was the result of a visit to England in 1862. He died in March 1893.

Flora Tristan
French Feminist, Socialist and Author

Flora Tristan was born in Paris in April 1803. Tristan campaigned for social justice for French workers, and for equality for women. She travelled around France in an attempt to set up a national workers' union and visited England several times to investigate the lives of the English poor. Her findings were recorded in *Promenades Dans Londres* published in 1842. She died in November 1844.

Thomas Wright
Engineer, School Inspector, Social Investigator and Author

Thomas Wright was born in Liverpool in April 1839, the son of a blacksmith. He completed an apprenticeship as an engineer and then worked as a blacksmith. In 1872 Wright became one of the first School Board Visitors appointed after the 1870 Education Act, a position he kept until he retired.

Wright wrote for *Cornhill* and *Fraser's Magazine* and *Continental Review*. His articles on the London poor were published in book form under the titles *Slum Homes of the Working Class* (1867), *The Great Unwashed* (1868) and *Our New Masters* (1873).

In his role as a school visitor, Wright became acquainted with the poor who lived in slum homes along the banks of the River Thames. Under the pseudonym of 'The Riverside Visitor', he wrote about his experiences in *Some Habits and Customs of the Working Classes* (1867), *The Great Army of the London Poor* (1882) and *The Pinch of Poverty* (1892). Wright died in February 1909.

Bibliography

Note on Sources

A number of primary sources have been found on www.victorian london.org, a vast resource on Victorian London containing the texts of many books now out of print or difficult to obtain.

Official Papers

Criminal and Destitute Juveniles, Select Committee on, 1852, Vol. V11

Private Letter

Charles Dickens to Elizabeth Gaskell, 31.1.1850

Books, Articles, Newspapers and Periodicals

Anon, *The Queen's London: A Pictorial and Descriptive Record of the Streets, Buildings, Parks and Scenery of the Great Metropolis in the Fifty-Ninth Year of the Reign of Her Majesty Queen Victoria, 1896* (victorianlondon.org)

Archer, Thomas, *The Pauper, the Thief and the Convict*, 1865 (Dodo Press Reprint, 2009)

Archer, Thomas, *The Terrible Sights of London*, 1870 (victorianlondon.org)

Barnardo, Mrs and Marchant, James, *Memoirs of the Late Dr Barnardo*, 1907 (Kessinger Legacy Reprint, 2009)

Booth, William, *In Darkest England and the Way Out,* 1890 (Salvation Army Social Services Centenary Edition, 1984)

Clout, Hugh (editor), *The Times London History Atlas* (Book Club Associates, 1991)

Continental Monthly Magazine, October 1862

Cunningham, Hugh, *The Invention of Childhood* (BBC Books, 2006)

Davey, Cyril, *A Man For All Children – The Story of Thomas Bowman Stephenson* (Epworth Press, 1968)

Davin, Anna, *Growing Up Poor* (Rivers Oram Press, 1996)

Dickens, Charles, *Reprinted Pieces* (P. R. Gawthorn, undated)

Dickens, Charles, *Shops and Tenants, Sketches by Boz* (www.victorianlondon.org)

Doré, Gustave and Jerrold, Blanchard, *London: A Pilgrimage,* 1872 (Dover Publications, 1970)

Duckworth, Jeannie, *Fagin's Children – Criminal Children in Victorian England* (Hambledon and London, 2002)

Engels, Friedrich, *The Condition of the Working Class in England,* 1845 (Lawrence and Wishart reprint, 1973)

Ewing Ritchie, James, *Here and There in London,* 1859 (victorianlondon.org)

Ewing Ritchie, James, *About London,* 1860 (victorianlondon.org)

Fisher, Trevor, *Prostitution and the Victorians* (Sutton Publishing, 1997)

Fried, Albert and Elman, Richard (editors), *Charles Booth's London: A Portrait of the Poor at the Turn of the Century Drawn from his Life and Labour of the People in London* (Pelican Books, 1971)

Godwin, George, *London Shadows. A Glance at the "Homes" of the Thousands,* 1854 (victorianlondon.org)

Grant, James, *Sketches in London,* 1838 (victorianlondon.org)

Grant, James, *Lights and Shadows of London Life*, 1842 (victorianlondon.org)

Greenwood, James, *The Seven Curses of London*, 1869 (Kessinger Rare Reprint, undated)

Greenwood, James, *Unsentimental Journeys Through Modern Babylon* (Ward, Lock and Taylor, 1867)

Hibbert, Christopher, *London; The Biography of a City* (Penguin Books, 1977)

Hibbert, Christopher, *The English, A Social History 1066–1945* (Grafton Books, 1987)

Hibbert, Christopher, *The Illustrated London News Social History of Victorian Britain* (Book Club Associates, 1975)

Hogg, Ethel, *Quintin Hogg – A Biography* (Archibald Constable and Co., 1904)

Hollingshead, John, *Ragged London in 1861* (J. M. Dent and Sons, 1986)

Horn, Pamela, *Children's Work and Welfare 1780–1880s* (Macmillan, 1994)

Horn, Pamela, *The Victorian and Edwardian Schoolchild* (Sutton Publishing, 1989)

Horn, Pamela, *The Victorian Town Child* (Sutton Publishing, 1997)

Howat, Irene and Nicholls, John, *Streets Paved With Gold, The Story of the London City Mission* (Christian Focus Publications, 2003)

Illustrated London News, 18.9.1852

Jackson, Lee, *Victorian London* (New Holland Publishers, 2004)

Keating, Peter, *Into Unknown England 1866–1913, Selections from the Social Explorers* (Fontana, 1976)

Leisure Hour, 1858 (victorianlondon.org)

Lewis, John, *London The Autobiography* (Constable and Robinson, 2008)

May, Trevor, *The Victorian Schoolroom* (Shire Publications, 1995)

Mayhew Henry, *London Labour and the London Poor*, 1851 (Penguin, 1985 – Victor Neuberg editor)

Mayhew, Henry and Binny, John, *The Criminal Prisons of London and Scenes of Prison Life*, 1862 (Nabu Public Domain Reprints, 2010)

Mayhew, Henry, *The Morning Chronicle Survey of Labour and the Poor; The Metropolitan Districts*, 1849–50 (Caliban Books, 1980)

Metcalf, Priscilla, *Victorian London* (Cassell, 1972)

Munby, Arthur, *Diary 1862* (victorianlondon.org)

Nead, Lynda, *Victorian Babylon – People, Streets and Images in Nineteenth Century London* (Yale University Press, 2000)

O'Daniel, W., *Ins and Outs of London*, 1859 (victorianlondon.org)

Owen, Roger J., *The National Children's Home* (Religious and Moral Education Press, 1985)

Payn, James, *Light and Shadows of London Life*, 1867 (victorianlondon.org)

Philip, Neil and Neuburg, Victor, *Charles Dickens – A December Vision and Other Thoughtful Writings* (Continuum Publishing Group, 1987)

Picard, Liza, *Victorian London – The Life of a City 1840–1870* (Weidenfeld and Nicolson, 2005)

Pollock, John, *Shaftesbury the Reformer* (Kingsway Publications, 2000)

Prochaska, Frank, *Women and Philanthropy in 19th Century England* (Clarendon Press, 1980)

Punch, July to December 1842

Quennell, Peter, *London's Underworld* (Selections from Volume 4 of Henry Mayhew's *London Labour and the London Poor*) (Bracken Books, 1983)

Quennell, Peter, *Mayhew's Characters* (Selections from Volumes 1–3 of Henry Mayhew's *London Labour and the London Poor*) (Spring Books, undated)

Rice-Jones, Revd D., *In the Slums,* 1884 (Dodo Press reprint, 2010)

Rose, June, *For the Sake of the Children – Inside Dr Barnardo's: 120 Years of Caring for Children* (Hodder and Stoughton, 1987)

Rowe, Richard, *Episodes in an Obscure Life,* 1871 (victorianlondon.org)

Rowe, Richard, *Life in the London Streets: Or Struggles For Daily Bread,* 1881 (Kessinger Legacy Reprint, undated)

Schlesinger, Max, *Saunterings In and Around London,* 1853 (victorianlondon.org)

Sheppard, Francis, *London 1808–1870: The Infernal Wen* (Secker and Warburg, 1971)

Sims, George, *How the Poor Live,* 1883 (victorianlondon.org)

Taine, Hippolyte, *Notes on England,* 1860 (Thames and Hudson, 1957)

Thomson, John and Smith, Adolphe, *Street Life in London,* 1877 (Reprinted by Dover Publications as *Victorian London Street Life in Historic Photographs,* 1994)

Thompson, E. P. and Yeo, Eileen, *The Unknown Mayhew* (Pelican Books, 1971)

The Times, 23.12.1864 (victorianlondon.org)

Tristan, Flora, *Promenades Dans Londres* (translated by Jean Hawkes as *The London Journal of Flora Tristan,* Virago, 1982)

'Uncle Jonathan', *Walks In and Around London,* 1895 (victorianlondon.org)

Vallance, Rosalind, *Dickens London,* selected essays of Charles Dickens (Folio Society, 1966)

Waifs and Strays Society, *The First Forty Years: A Chronicle of the Church of England Waifs and Strays Society 1881–1920,* (SPCK, 1922)

Walvin, James, *A Child's World: A History of English Childhood 1800–1914* (Pelican Books, 1982)

Weightman, Gavin and Humphries, Steve, *The Making of Modern London* (Sidgwick and Jackson, 1983)

Weinreb, Ben and Hibbert, Christopher (editors), *The London Encyclopedia* (Book Club Associates, 1983)

White, Jerry, *London in the Nineteenth Century, A Human Awful Wonder of God* (Jonathan Cape, 2007)

Wright, Thomas, *The Great Army of the London Poor* (victorianlondon.org)

Wright, Thomas, *The Pinch of Poverty*, 1892 (victorianlondon.org))

Website

www.redhill-reigate-history.co.uk/philanthanth.htm (Royal Philanthropic Society)

Index

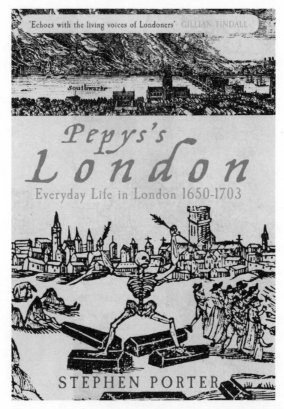

Also available from Amberley Publishing

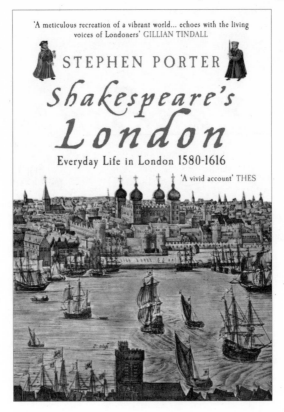

Everyday life in the teeming metropolis during William Shakespeare's time in the city (c.1580-1616), the height of Queen Elizabeth I's reign

'A vivid account' THES

'A lucid and cogent narrative of everyday life' SHAKESPEARE BIRTHPLACE TRUST

Shakespeare's London was a bustling, teeming metropolis that was growing so rapidly that the government took repeated, and ineffectual, steps to curb its expansion. From contemporary letters, journals and diaries, a vivid picture emerges of this fascinating city, with its many opportunities and also its persistent problems.

£9.99 Paperback
127 illustrations (45 colour)
304 pages
978-1-84868-200-9

Available from all good bookshops or to order direct
Please call **01453-847-800**
www.amberleybooks.com

Also available from Amberley Publishing

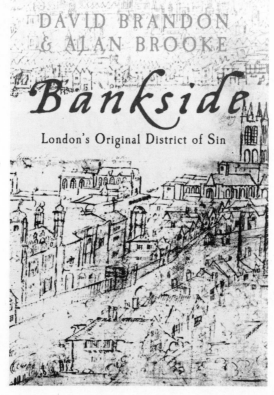

The story of historic district on the south bank of the Thames and beyond - the original playground of Londoners, complete with inns, bear pits, brothels and theatres

From a time when London was a collection of discrete districts and villages, here is the long history of Bankside, the metropolis's disreputable and licentious yet vibrant, cosmopolitan underbelly.

£20 Hardback
79 illustrations (41 colour)
304 pages
978-1-84868-336-5

Available from all good bookshops or to order direct
Please call **01453-847-800**
www.amberleybooks.com